TEN PROPHECIES FOR THE DEMISE OF ISRAEL 2022

HANCHI NACEUR

TEN PROPHECIES FOR THE DEMISE
OF ISRAEL 2022

TABLE OF CONTENT

1

INTRODUCTION

This book is based on diverse sources and researches and includes 10 different and detailed prophecies. Some of them are from the Holy Quran {*Falsehood cannot approach it from before it or from behind it; [it is] a revelation from a [Lord who is] Wise and Praiseworthy*} [Fussilat: 42]. Others are from the Torah and the Bible, despite having been subject of distortion, some are astronomical and others are environmental or topographical, which, for example, we see at firsthand as when looking in Lake Tiberias with unprecedented lack of water level. All the aforementioned confirm and forewarn of the end of the State of Israel.

It is also a message of love, an omen and a warning.

A message telling those who do evil to stop their harming, as Beit Al-Maqdis and its surroundings, are considered a blessed land owned by the Unitarians (Al-Muwahhidoun), who followed Moses and Jesus and Muhammad (PBUT) and did not differentiate between them. There is no difference between an Arab or a Jew (if the meaning is nationality) and non-Arab except piety.

It is also a warning message for those who are impatient in order to know that the whole thing is an act of Allah and all falls in its hands; Almighty says, {*So be not impatient over them. We only count out to them a [limited] number*} [Mariam: 84], the when, where and how, everything happens upon the will of Allah and within a specific time that cannot be either delayed nor taken earlier in terms of place and time except with His permission, blessed be his names the all-knowing and the Aware. So let's opt for no assault, no abuse and no terror; even if you believe that you are a right holder.

It is also a third message to those who are vulnerable, telling them to be patient, enduring, holding still and not abusing. Be like a fruitful tree to which people throw stones but rewards them with fruits.

The Core of the Book:

It is about 10 prophecies or signs of the demise of Israel that we may be almost sure of its occurrence for the abundance of evidence and the diversity of their sources. But we cannot guarantee that it will occur in its deadlines because the unseen will remain unseen unless it occurs. However, it is almost indisputable for the abundance of evidence, arguments and proofs.

I have focused and elaborated on the Quranic evidence of its truthfulness and accuracy, as well as the Gematria and the numerical miracles in the Quran to illustrate the language of numbers, calculation and logic, the inevitability of the demise of Israel in the Quran.

Note:

I apologize to the readers for having repeated some information in some chapters knowing that the intention is to let information or idea take root in your minds. In addition, the book is edited using two languages so that the reader can be sure of the original, because it is difficult or impossible to translate some meanings. That's why I deliberately preserved the Arabic text in every translation so that the non-Arab readers can verify the original if needed.

I would like to point out in this introduction that we asked for

the authorization and collaboration of Noon Center for Quranic Studies and their reply is as below with many thanks

By The name of Allah the Merciful

Dear Brother Naceur AL – HANCHI,

May Allah's peace, mercy and blessings be upon you,

Thanks for your interest asking His Almighty to bless you in your efforts,

There is no problem to quote in any way for a brother who keen to do good and deliver the main idea of Islam,

May Allah supports you and keeps you on the straight way,

Noon for Quranic Studies,

From: Naceur Hanchi mailto:

naceur.hanchi@hotmail.com

Sent: Monday, April 04, 2016 7:16 AM

To: noon@p-ol.com

PREFACE

Introduction to Gematria

Why Gematria?

Gematria is a tool we must understand to explore some of the secrets of the Quran by giving numerical value to the letters of the Arabic alphabet. The purpose is to draw logical results and mystical secrets that are possible in the Quran, but are hidden from us between the letters and words of the latter and their numbers and numerical and arithmetic value. The Almighty Creator wants us to look, study, learn and explore some of the Quran's instruments. Meanwhile, let us know that the Quran's Gematria is a fact that needs to be examined and adopted as a mechanism for the search for the inevitability of the demise of Israel in the Holy Quran.

Dr, Bassam JARRAR, Discoverer of the Numerical Miracles in Quran 2022

Gematria is a new old science. It can be tracked in language as well as in history back to the pre-Islamic period by 1300 years. It has been proved to be entirely true and compatible with the Quran in Ottoman script. You are even surprised by the writing of some words in the Quran differently than as articulated such as the word (إسرائيل) which is written without (Alif) (اسرئيل) and the word (وكذلك نجي) written as (وكذلك نجي) or as His Almighty said: {*Indeed, it is We who sent down the Quran and indeed, We will be its guardian*} [AL-Hijr: 9], the word (الحفظون) is written without prolongation letter.

Many others are in the Holy Quran and the secret in that is to be consistent with the Gematria and the numerical miracle. Therefore, Dr. Bassam JARRAR said that the Quran relies on Gematria and we will draw evidence from it later in the chapter of the demise of Israel in Quran, Sabbaths and others.

Arabic alphabets consist of 29 characters, but the alphabet is 28 characters, since there is no difference in the alphabet between A and Hamza. Here, we are concerned with the alphabetical order, and the correlation of this order with the so-called Gematria, which is used in the Semitic languages. Hence, we find that the Hebrew alphabet corresponds to the Arabic alphabet until the letter (ت), and the Arabic exceeds with: (غ، ظ، ض، ذ، خ، ث).

It is not easy to know the alphabetical order basis and that of the calculation that was associated to it in the Semitic languages; as there are many statements in this sense, so it is difficult to assert or weight. This calculation may have a religious basis; Jewish clerics use it a lot, Muslims have used it in history, and the Sufis has exaggerated using it, as did the people of witchcraft, priesthood and sorcery. It is not excluded, as we have mentioned, that this calculation has a religious basis, then has been affected by distortion, substitution and bad employment.

The alphabetical order in the Maghreban north differs slightly from that of the old and modern one, which is: (Abjad, Huz, Hatti, Kalman, Saafis, Qurasht, Thakhth, Dhazgh). The Hebrew alphabet, as we have said, ends with "Qurasht". Each letter is given a numerical value as follow:

أ	1	ي	10	ق	100	غ	1000
ب	2	ك	20	ر	200		
ج	3	ل	30	ش	300		
د	4	م	40	ت	400		
ه	5	ن	50	ث	500		
و	6	س	60	خ	600		
ز	7	ع	70	ذ	700		
ح	8	ف	80	ض	800		
ط	9	ص	90	ظ	900		

We notice that there is complete consistency and equivalence between the Arabic letters of the alphabet from the first letter (أ) to (غ) and the arithmetic numbers from (1) to thousand (1000), as it includes the one, double, triple digits and closes completely at thousand with the letter (غ), which is surprisingly nice as if it suggests the Who created the Arabic characters is the creator of the numbers as well as the law between them which implicates a lot of secrets. You also notice that if you add the numerical value of the letters from (أ) to (غ) you will get a total value of 5995, i.e.:

$$أ+ب+ج+..+ط+....+ق+....غ = + 1+ 2+ 3 +... 10 ...+ 100 +... 1000$$
$$= 5995$$

If 5995 is calculated as follows: $5 + 9 + 9 + 5$ we get the number 28, which is exactly equal to the Arabic alphabet 28 characters and this implicates mysteries.

In the Gematria, it is noticed that there is no difference in the numerical value between the (أ) and (ع), being based on the alphabet, not the spelling. This calculation has been used for many purposes; Muslims used it in the histography of battles, deaths, buildings, etc. ...such as:

When the Sultan (Barqouq), a sultan of the Circassians dynasty, died, some funny and nice people drew up an expression specifying the date of his death as: (في المشمش "in apricots"). In that way, the death of Barqouq is in apricots (في المشمش). The numerical value of this expression is: 801 = (300 + 40 + 300 + 40 + 30 + 1 + 10 + 80), and therefore the death of Sultan (Barqouq) was on 801 AH.

Another Example:

A poet (named Dalangawi) died, and a friend of his mourned him indicating the date of his death, he said:

> I asked the poem do you have a friend
>> As Dalangawi entered his grave
> It cried and fell unconscious
>> Then lied in the grave with him
> I said to those who asks for the poem to be short
>> I have indicated the date: the poem died after he's gone

The poet gave a key word to show us how to count, where he said: (I have indicated the date) i.e., calculate the phrase that comes after the expression (I have indicated the date). The poet could have used other words in which the meaning of arithmetic, counting, or history, or words referring to the sentence that carries the numerical value desired by the poet. In this example, the words: (مات الشعر بعده) indicates the date of Dalangawi death:

(1123 AH) = (40 + 1 + 400 + 1 + 30 + 300 + 70 + 200 + 2 + 70 + 4 + 5).

It is clear that the use of this calculation in history is appropriate from the legitimate point of view, because it is like terminology. However, the use of Gematria in magic, sorcery, priesthood, and astrology, has harmed this innocent calculation method.

Note:

Please see the appendix for the explanation and download directives of Gematria program for the Holy Quran from internet.

Numerical Miracles in Quran and Gematria

What is the Numerical Miracle?

Here are briefly three examples:

1. First Example:

Surat Al Hadid (The Iron); the name of the surah: Al-Hadid, its number is (57) out of 114 Surah in all the Quran, i.e., half of the Quran.

Now, let's apply the Gematria on the word الحديد according to the previous table as follow:

ا+ل+ح+د+ي+د, is: 1+30+8+4+10+4 = **57** and this is the average atomic weight of the iron agreed on scientifically. 55, 56, 57, 58, 59 and others are called iron isotopes.

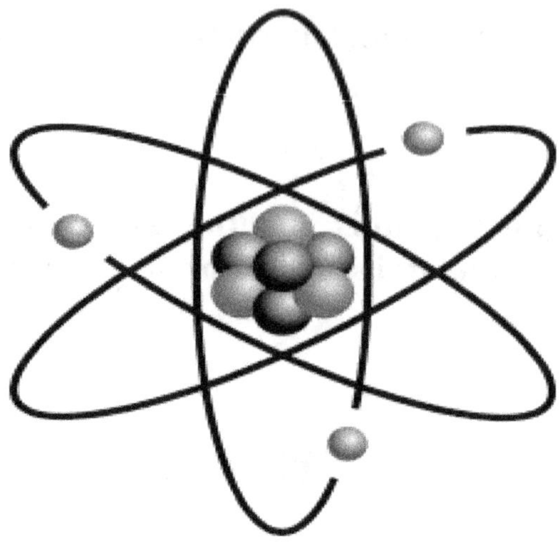

Lithium Atom

It consists of a nucleus containing 3 <u>protons</u> and 4 <u>neutrons</u>, and surrounded by 3 <u>electrons</u> moving in orbits.

Moreover, if we delete the first two letters from the word iron in Arabic, the word becomes "حديد" i.e.: (ح+د+ي+د) = 4+10+4+ 8 = 26 which is the atomic number of the iron, i.e. the number of electrons in the iron atom is 26. What is remarkable in the Quran is that the verse in which the word iron is mentioned in Surat Al-Hadid if calculated starting from Basmalah is the verse number 26.

2. Second example:

Surat Al-Kahf (The Cave), the number of this Surah in the Holy Quran is 18. The noteworthy here is that the story of the cave people in the same surah is told in 18 verses starting from the words of His Almighty: {*Or have you thought that the companions of the cave and the inscription were, among Our signs, a wonder?}* [Al-Kahf: 9] till *{And they remained in their cave for three hundred years and exceeded by nine}* [Al-Kahf: 25]

The number of words from the first word about the story{أم} till the word {ثلاث} in the "verse 25" equals 309 words and the same number is the duration of their stay in the cave which is 309 years .. By calculating the words from the word {لبثوا} the first mentioned «verse 12» till the word {ولبثوا} «verse 25», the surprise is that the exact number of words is "309" which is equal to what they spent in their cave.

3. Third example:

The Almighty says in surat Al-Ankaboot about Noah, (PBUH): *{and he remained among them a thousand years minus fifty years}* [Al-Ankaboot: 14]; if the meaning of this Holy verse is: Noah, (PBUH), stayed among his people (950) years, The Almighty mentioned the words سنة and عام (year) in one verse, so what is the secret?

The answer:

Scientists believe that the use of the word سنة in the Quran means the solar year and the word عام means the lunar year.

Astronomers divide the solar year into an (astral) year amounting for (365,25636) days and an (Orbital) year amounting for (365,2422) days. If we take the average of the astral and orbital years, the number of days of (1000) years is (365249) days. The astronomers also divide the lunar year into an (astral) year amounting for (327,85992) days, and an (orbital) year amounting for (354,36707) days. Same, if we take the average of the astral and orbital years, the number of days of (50) years is (17056) days. Now we can do the subtraction as follow (365249-17056) = 348193 days, which corresponds to (953,3) orbital years and (953,28) astral years.

Thus, it is clear that the period he remained in the cave, peace be upon him, was (953) years not (950) as understood at first sight.

Do we have a numerical evidence for this finding?

a. In the Holy Quran, the Surah No. (71) is (Noah), so what is the relationship between this surah and the time he remained, peace be upon him, in the cave and the result we got before? The reader is surprised when counting the number of letters in the Surah of (Noah) amounting for (953) characters, which is equal to his stay duration, (PBUH) Is all of this a coincidence? Never, there is no coincidence in the Book of Allah. The Almighty said: {*Indeed, all things We created with predestination*} [Al-Qamar: 49] and He said: {*We have not neglected in the Register a thing*} [Al-Ana'am: 38]

After ascertaining that the Holy Quran contains numerical miracle and relies on Gematria, we will take a break and move to the chapter of Sabbaths, to address the demise of Israel in the Holy Quran, the number 76 and other topics.

<u>Return to the table</u>

The Jews Lurking the Red Heifer as a Condition for Building the Temple

We recall this section in the introduction to know that the project of the demolition of Beit-Al-Maqdis and the building of the Temple is a fact and all necessary Talmudic doctrine, technical and material potentials are been prepared for it. This is very critical and if people go ahead with this act and destroy the Holy Beit-Al-Maqdis unjustly and aggressively, then they would go into a path of no return.

A black spot has been discovered on this Heifer and then was abandoned

The red heifer, which is lurked by the Jews as a condition before the practical construction of the temple, must be 100% red. When it is found and sealed, it will be slaughtered then purified with as we will see below.

A bomb on all fours:

The Israeli journalist (David Landau) warned the Israeli security services in (Haartez) Newspaper about the terrible danger that may result from the story of the red heifer telling them that it is not an ordinary cow; it is rather, a time bomb on all fours and so, it outweigh any terrorist as it can start a huge fire in the entire Middle East, simply because it is a weapon equivalent to any non-conventional weapon or bomb. They say that David Landau is a pacifist, so he quickly realized that the emergence of the so-called Red Heifer could evoke in the Jews the old repressed desires of building the Temple in the site of the Haram al-Sharif, leading to ignite the war between Israel and the whole Muslim world as well as Indonesia. The Jews have put the red heifer in a separate place and left it under the guard of a dog who failed to protect it from the infiltration of white hair into the scalp of its red body. They claim that it was red and must be slaughtered and burned outside the temple until it coalesces and turns into ashes. The Jews claim that the Temple has been destroyed since 1900 years, but its location is spotted above the Mountain of God at a distance of 35 acres in the old city of Jerusalem, the site of Al-Haram Al-Sharif which is no longer looking like a mount because the great King Herod, Judea's king in the first century before Christ was the one who enlarged the temple courtyard over the top of a hill called Moriah. According to their legends, only the western wall, which they call the Wailing Wall, where Jews shed tears over the destruction of the Temple stood still.

So as to not prolong the talk, here are some pictures.

This is the first gold candlestick made since the destruction of the second Temple some 2,000 years ago ... It is called in Hebrew (Menorah…). It is now preserved meters away from Al-Aqsa in a Jewish office called the Temple Mount Institute ... which is visited by thousands of Jews every day to learn about what was completed in the preparation for the construction of the temple knowing that the Institute is a governmental institution established by the Israeli government.

This is the red Heifer (Melody ...) which was born in the north of Palestine and Jews believe that its birth is a sign from Allah that it is time to build the Temple and that the ashes of this Heifer will purify the people of Israel as a prelude before entering the Temple.

These golden cups were made to be used for the feast of water purification.

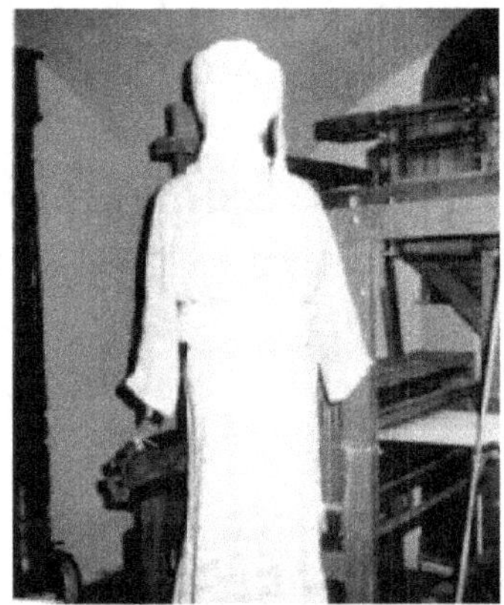

This is what the Temple monks and junior priests will wear

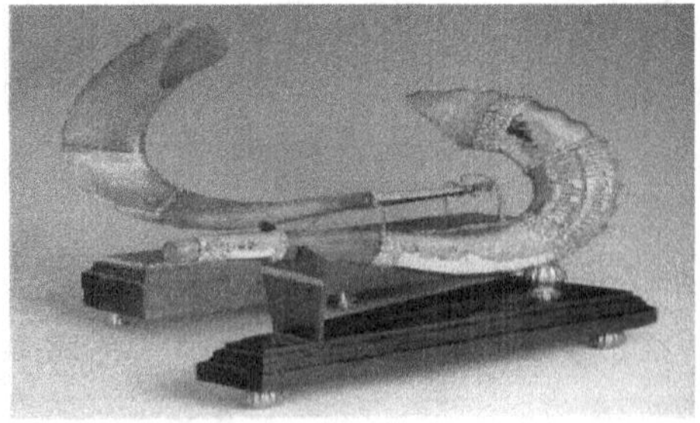

Bull Horns, one golden in which priests are buffering in their festivals and the second silver buffered in to announce the time of fasting

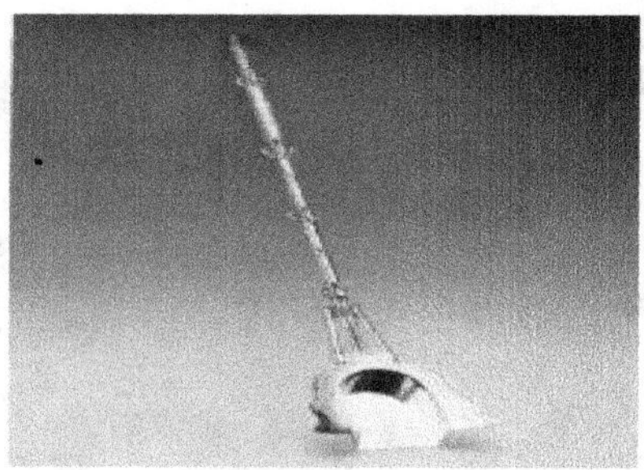

The silver shovel which priests will use to remove the offerings ashes from the altar

A guitar made for the Temple according to the biblical description; it has 22 chords as the number of Hebrew alphabet

The holy seals which distinguish the offerings that will be slaughtered

Purity pot

A picture of the golden altar surrounded by silver trumpets that are played in seasons

These golden and silver knives are the ones that the priests will use to sacrifice offerings

The Temple stone ready for construction

This is a model of what the Temple will be like

According to (Jörnberg), what the Jews call by the Temple Mount is now **Al-Haram Al-Sharif, third Holiest Mosques for Muslims. Near its center is (the Dome of the Rock), from which the Prophet, (PBUH) ascended to heaven in the night of Isra and Mi'raj.**

While Ben-Gurion's Life:

Gorenberg goes further back, and says: Israeli forces managed to enter and occupy Jerusalem at 9 am on June 7, 1967, on the third day of the Six-Day War. Since then, Jerusalem's Al-haram al-Sharif has been under Jewish rule for the first time since 70 AD.

Nevertheless, the leaders of Israel (Eshkol and Dayan) decided while Ben-Gurion's life that Al-Aqsa Mosque and al-Haram al-Sharif should remain in the hands of Arab Muslims in Jerusalem.

Ben-Gurion,

Stood by this decision in order to prevent Israel from the risk of getting into the holy war. The Jews were always keen to perform the pilgrimage only to the Western Wall knowing that the rabbis of Israel unanimously refused to allow any Jew to enter the gates of Al-Haram Al-Sharif, because the laws of Jewish religion confirm that Jews cannot be purified of contact with dead people in the absence of the red heifer's ashes and therefore, cannot enter the sacred field. The great rabbi of Israel said: "The Temple cannot be built before the Lord sends the Christ back in a future day. Until that happens, every believing Jew should pray to the Lord and wait. The rabbis also emphasized that the success of the Israeli army in occupying Jerusalem was not enough to build the Temple".

(Gorenberg) stresses:

(That at the end of the year 2000 if the future does not come now, if Jews waiting period does not end and if history does not go towards the end height, the prophecies of the Torah come true before our eyes).

Gorenberg mentions, regarding the place of the last events, that the idea of resurrection exists in Islam, Christianity and Judaism, and Muslims who believe that Israel's occupation of the Holy Jerusalem is a declaration from heaven that the hour is near. Meanwhile, the believers of Biblical texts of Torah and Talmud affirm that al-Quds or Jerusalem is where the last major events will take place on earth and that the Haram Al-Sharif is the location of the Lord's Mountain, the center of these events and the center of the end of the world.

Proponents of the extreme Israeli religious right assert that every passing day since June 1967 is a lost opportunity to rebuild the Temple, the site of Haram al-Sharif while Christians in the American extreme religious right believe that the construction of the Temple by the Jews is a necessary condition for the return of Christ or the second coming of Christ. In contrast, according to Gorenberg; Muslims believe that Jews attempt to destroy Al-Aqsa Mosque is one of the resurrection signs.

Return to the table

THE FIRST PROPHECY

The demise of Israel in the Torah and the Bible

It is stated in Leviticus, Chapter (25): The Lord said to Moses at Mount Sinai, "Speak to the Israelites and say to them: 'When you enter the land I am going to give you, the land itself must observe a sabbath to the Lord. For six years sow your fields, and for six years prune your vineyards and gather their crops. But in the seventh year the land is to have a year of sabbath rest, a sabbath to the Lord. Do not sow your fields or prune your vineyards. Do not reap what grows of itself or harvest the grapes of your untended vines. The land is to have a year of rest". After the detailed provisions of this seventh year law, he says in Chapter 26: "... But if you will not listen to me and carry out all these commands, and if you reject my decrees and abhor my laws and fail to carry out all my commands and so violate my covenant, then I will do this to you: I will bring on you sudden terror... I will scatter you among the nations and will draw out my sword and pursue you. Your land will be laid waste, and your cities will lie in ruins. Then the land will enjoy its sabbath years all the time that it lies desolate and you are in the country of your enemies; then the land will rest and enjoy its sabbaths. All the time that it lies desolate, the land will have the rest it did not have during the sabbaths you lived in it…".

The demise of Israel from the Torah and Bible books

The commandment of Moses, peace be upon him, which was not carried out by the children of Israel and the result comes from the Book of Deuteronomy, which states: "Assemble before me all the elders of your tribes and all your officials, so that I can speak these words in their hearing and call the heavens and the earth to testify against them ❋ For I know that after my death you are sure to become utterly corrupt and to turn from the way I have commanded you. In days to come, disaster will fall on you because you will do evil in the sight of the Lord and arouse his anger by what your hands have made." 31/28, 29.

The Free Jews demanding the right of the Palestinians to their land, their country and their holy sites

The end of Israel in the Battle of the Promise of the Hereafter (called Armageddon Battle or Valley of

Megiddo), which gathers the world armies in Palestine and this is what was stated in the book of Ezekiel: The word of the Lord came to me: "Son of man, set your face against Gog, of the land of Magog, the chief prince of Meshek and Tubal ❋ prophesy against him and say: 'This is what the Sovereign Lord says: I am against you, Gog, chief prince of Meshek and Tubal ❋ I will turn you around, put hooks in your jaws and bring you out with your whole army—your horses, your horsemen fully armed, and a great horde with large and small shields, all of them brandishing their swords. Persia, Cush and Put will be with them, all with shields and helmets ❋ also Gomer with all its troops, and Beth Togarmah from the far north with all its troops—the many nations with you ❋ Get ready; be prepared, you and all the hordes gathered about you, and take command of them After ❋ many days you will be called to arms. In future years you will invade a land that has recovered from war, whose people were gathered from many nations to the mountains of Israel, which had long been desolate. They had been brought out from the nations, and now all of them live in safety ❋ You and all your troops and the many nations with you will go up, advancing like a storm". Chapter 38/1:9.

The Meaning of the Country names according to the Scholar Wilhelm Gesenius (1786-1842) Researcher in Ancient Semitic Languages and Discoverer of Phoenician Grammar:

- **Meshek: one of Japheth's sons and it is the word from which the name of Moscow was derived.**
- **Rush: the name of the son of our Prophet Jacob's youngest son Benjamin, and the origin of the word Russia.**
- **Tubal: Tibolsk (Belarus), the area between the Black Sea and the Caspian Sea.**

- **Persia: Iran.**
- **Cush: Al-Habasha (Ethiopia).**
- **Put: Libya.**
- **Gomer: Eastern Europe.**
- **Togarmah: Turkey, specifically: the area located on the Caspian Sea.**

From the Far North:

Most of those countries especially: Meshek, Topal, Togarmah, Gog and Magog are from the Far North.

The reasons for the demise of Israel from Ezekiel's Book are as follows: "This is what the Sovereign Lord says: This is Jerusalem, which I have set in the center of the nations, with countries all around her ✸Yet in her wickedness she has rebelled against my laws and decrees more than the nations and countries around her. She has rejected my laws and has not followed my decrees ✸Therefore this is what the Sovereign Lord says: You have been more unruly than the nations around you and have not followed my decrees or kept my laws. You have not even conformed to the standards of the nations around you ✸Therefore this is what the Sovereign Lord says: I myself am against you, Jerusalem, and I will inflict punishment on you in the sight of the nations ✸ Because of all your detestable idols, I will do to you what I have never done before and will never do again ✸ Therefore in your midst parents will eat their children, and children will eat their parents. I will inflict punishment on you and will scatter all your survivors to the winds". Chapter 5/5:10.

Other reasons for the demise of Israel are concluded as well from Ezekiel's Book: "The word of the Lord came to me ✳ Son of man, this is what the Sovereign Lord says to the land of Israel: The end! The end has come upon the four corners of the land! ✳ The end is now upon you, and I will unleash my anger against you. I will judge you according to your conduct and repay you for all your detestable practices ✳ I will not look on you with pity; I will not spare you. I will surely repay you for your conduct and for the detestable practices among you. Then you will know that I am the Lord ✳ For the land is full of bloodshed, and the city is full of violence ✳ I will bring the most wicked of nations to take possession of their houses. I will put an end to the pride of the mighty, and their sanctuaries will be desecrated ✳ When terror comes, they will seek peace in vain ✳ Calamity upon calamity will come, and rumor upon rumor". Chapter 7/1:25

The Battle of Armageddon was also described in the book of Zechariah: "On that day the weeping in Jerusalem will be as great as the weeping of Hadad Rimmon in the plain of Megiddo ✳ The land will mourn, each clan by itself, with their wives by themselves: the clan of the house of David and their wives, the clan of the house of Nathan and their wives ✳ the clan of the house of Levi and their wives, the clan of Shimei and their wives ✳ and all the rest of the clans and their wives". Chapter 12/11:14

"Proclaim this among the nations: Prepare for war! Rouse the warriors! Let all the fighting men draw near and attack ✳ Beat your plowshares into swords and your pruning hooks into spears ✳ Let the weakling say, I am strong! ❋ Come quickly, all you nations from every side ❋ and assemble there". Joel Book, 3/9:11

Thus: Jihad and Entrust, according to preparation.

Jeremiah's Book urges on racing time and destructing the state of luxury and the community of violence: "So arise, let us attack at night ❋ and destroy her fortresses! ❋ This is what the Lord Almighty says ❋ Cut down the trees; and build siege ramps against Jerusalem ❋This city must be punished; it is filled with oppression ❋ As a well pours out its water ❋ So she pours out her wickedness ❋ Violence and destruction resound in her ❋ Her sickness and wounds are ever before me ❋ Look, an army is coming; from the land of the north ❋ A great nation is being stirred up from the ends of the earth ❋ They are armed with bow and spear ❋They are cruel and show no mercy ❋ They sound like the roaring sea ❋ As they ride on their horses;
they come like men in battle formation ❋ To attack you, Daughter Zion". 6/4:7-22:23

...And pray, so that your escape would not be in winter or in the Sabbath, for it shall be then...

"and inscribe it on a scroll ❋ That for the days to come ❋ It may be an everlasting witness ❋ Because you have rejected this message ❋ Relied on oppression ❋ and depended on deceit ❋ this sin will become for you ❋ like a high wall, cracked and bulging, that collapses suddenly, in an instant ❋ It will break in pieces like pottery, shattered so mercilessly that among its pieces ❋ not a fragment will be found for taking coals from a hearth ❋ or scooping water out of a cistern." Isaiah, 30/8:12-14

"A thousand will flee at the threat of one ✺ at the threat of five you will all flee away ✺ till you are left like a flagstaff on a mountaintop ✺ like a banner on a hill." Isaiah, 30/17. The book of Amos confirmed it: "The time is ripe ✺ for my people Israel; ✺ I will spare them no longer ✺ In that day," declares the Sovereign Lord, the songs in the temple will turn to wailing ✺ Many, many bodies ✺ flung everywhere! Silence!" Amos, 8/2:3

As for the characteristics of Al-Mujahideen, Joel depicted them in a very creative manner:
"Like dawn spreading across the mountains ✺ a large and mighty army comes ✺ such as never was in ancient times ✺ nor ever will be in ages to come ✺ Before them fire devours ✺ behind them a flame blazes ✺ Before them the land is like the garden of Eden ✺ Behind them, a desert waste ✺ Nothing escapes them ✺ They have the appearance of horses ✺ They gallop along like cavalry ✺ With a noise like that of chariots ✺ They leap over the mountaintops ✺ like a crackling fire consuming stubble ✺ like a mighty army drawn up for battle ✺ At the sight of them, nations are in anguish ✺ Every face turns pale ✺ They charge like warriors ✺ They scale walls like soldiers ✺ They all march in line ✺ Not swerving from their course ✺ They do not jostle each other ✺ Each marches straight ahead ✺ They plunge through defenses ✺ without breaking ranks ✺ They rush upon the city ✺ They run along the wall ✺ They climb into the houses ✺ They enter through the windows." 2/2:9

Isaiah describes them as follow:

"He lifts up a banner for the distant nations ✳ He whistles for those at the ends of the earth ✳ here they come, swiftly and speedily! ✳ Not one of them grows tired or stumbles ✳ Not one slumbers or sleeps ✳ Not a belt is loosened at the waist ✳ Not a sandal strap is broken ✳ Their arrows are sharp ✳ All their bows are strung ✳ Their horses' hooves seem like flint ✳ Their chariot wheels like a whirlwind ✳ Their roar is like that of the lion ✳ They roar like young lions ✳ They growl as they seize their prey ✳ And carry it off with no one to rescue ✳ In that day they will roar over it like the roaring of the sea ✳ And if one looks at the land ✳ There is only darkness and distress ✳ Even the sun will be darkened by clouds." 5/26:30.

Finally, a clear threat and a net promise remain in the Book of Deuteronomy:

"It came in the Book of Deuteronomy, fourth chapter, where the discourse was for Jews: After you have had children and grandchildren and have lived in the land a long time, if you then become corrupt and make any kind of idol, doing evil in the eyes of the Lord your God and arousing his anger; I call the heavens and the earth as witnesses against you this day that you will quickly perish from the land that you are crossing the Jordan to possess, you will not live there long but will certainly be destroyed, although the expected Child". 4/25:26.

<u>Return to the table</u>

* * *

THE SECOND PROPHECY

Three documents declare: Israel is in danger!

We often focus when writing about Israel, about common conflict issues, about its negotiations with the Palestinians, or about its terrorist operations against the civilian population. In the midst of this, we forget to look at the problems of Israel, especially those arising from the ongoing conflict, which negate the views of those who claim that resisting the occupation is absurd. In an attempt to make up for this shortcoming, we will take a quick look at three Israeli documents that have been discussed recently.

The first document:

Is a recent book released by the Intelligence man (Matti Steinberg), entitled "Stand against their destiny". The author is a former adviser to four heads of Israel Security Agency (Shin Bet), who started working in the agency in 1991.

The author talks about Israel's management of the negotiations and settlement process with the Palestinians and the Arabs. It stems from the basic idea that Israel must withdraw to the borders of June 4, 1967 in order to achieve a settlement that ensures long-term interests. He strongly criticizes the solution proposed by Ehud Barak to the late President Yasser Arafat in Camp David negotiations in 2000 and does strongly criticizes also Israel's rejection of the Arab Peace Initiative adopted at the Beirut Summit in 2002.

The author talks about the negotiations between Barak and Arafat and says: Barak adopted in his proposal for a settlement on the principle of withdrawal to the 1967 borders, but his offer included exceptions that undermine this principle, especially on the issue of Jerusalem and the area of the Holy Basin. The author states that he told Barak at the time that Arafat would not give up the effective sovereignty over the Holy Basin and would reject the existence of an Israeli flag. He says that Arafat was already afraid of turning Jerusalem into the "model" of Hebron, where Israel divided the Ibrahimi Mosque and controlled everything. The author told Barak at the time, too: that these gaps could break the negotiations, and warned him about putting Arafat before two options either to accept the dictates of Israel or blowing up the negotiations; but that was what Barak did in fact.

The author does not present these remarks as a technical advice, but rather for a vision he believes in. He believes that "Israel's abstention or avoidance of paying the price required for the settlement, which is the withdrawal to the 1967 borders", carries risks for the existence of the State of Israel as a democratic Jewish state much more than the risks of giving up some zones.

He declares then his strong support for the Arab Peace Initiative, and warns about the fact that "missing the chance to a two-state solution will take the conflict to another turn, which is the Palestinian demand (under the permanent occupation) for the rights of citizenship. This demand will grow and will find international support, and then its achievement would mean the end of Zionism; the end of the State of Israel we know".

In another context, the author criticizes Ariel Sharon's latest policy and supporters, which is based on the need for (suffering great hardship) the Arab situation to wake up and accept what Israel demands.

The policy was based on the slogan of (the lack of a partner for negotiation), and the policy of imposing an Israeli solution. Here, he says that the slogan of (suffering great hardship) was launched by the head of the Shin Bet six months after the launch of the Arab Peace Initiative, and says that Israel's rejection of the initiative proves that Israel is the one that needs (suffering great hardship). He says also that Barak and the executioners in the argument that there is no partner, such as Ariel Sharon and Shaul Mofaz, have caused unimaginable damage to Israel, because the end will be Israel's slide into the reality of a binational state suffering of calamities.

The second document:

A study published by the University of Haifa under the title of "The State of Tel Aviv: A Threat to Israel" by Professor Arnon Sofer. The study examines the dangers of misguided policies and self-destructive factors. It says: There is a global phenomenon characterized by the increasing size of the big cities and their demographic and economic growth against the interest of the parties due to migration and concentration of resources in those cities. He refers here to the uniqueness of the situation in Israel and its danger to the fact that the people of the center, i.e. Tel Aviv and its surroundings, are from Jews, while the inside Palestinians are concentrated in the edges. The study shows that the Israeli entity is getting less day by day and is confined to Tel Aviv area. The study says that the incursion of Jews at the heart of the state means a direct threat to them, endangering the entire Zionist project to a terrible chaos. He concludes with a remarkable conclusion in which he says: "If Israel continues to do so, it will implement its partition resolution of 1947, and its existence will be reduced to a coastal strip extending from Haifa to Ashkelon passing through Tel Aviv, and Israel will not be able to survive for a long time, stating the year 2020 as almost the beginning". Do Palestinians in the State of Israel have a role in this? The study answers this question by saying that "there is a great chance that Palestinian forces will be formed across the Green Line (i.e. between Israel and the West Bank), working together to establish a large Palestinian state". The study recognizes that the Palestinians in Israel consider the state as their enemy; it has turned them from a majority to a minority, deprived them of their rights, and continues to persecute them. The

study concludes that Palestinians in the State of Israel "witness a stage of national and religious extremism and see themselves as part of the Palestinian people". This conclusion is a new and strange concept of extremism; if the Palestinian citizen insists on his identity, he became then extremist and dangerous.

The third document:

A study published by Adva Center entitled (The Burden of the Israeli-Palestinian Conflict) by the editor professor Shlomo Sibirski. It examines the burden of conflict in eleven economic, social and military fields, and discusses the burden of conflict on facts, figures, percentages, and comparisons with previous Israeli times when calm was dominating.

The study argues that the conflict with the Palestinians is like a millstone on Israel's neck: it undermines its economic growth, burdens its budget, limits its social development, undermines its international standing, drains its army, and threatens its political space and its future existence as a Jewish nation-state. The study acknowledges that Israel is paying a heavy price as a result of the continuing conflict and the delay on implementing a solution based on a just and agreed division.

The study goes on basing on this theory examining the reality of the conflict burden in each field; for example, the increase in the defense budget (only the increase), about 37 billion between 1989 and 2008, exceeds the annual expenditure on the education system and the higher education system in Israel in 2008. Then, the cost of withdrawing from Gaza (compensations for settlers) was

NIS 9 billion and the cost of building the separation wall is NIS 13 billion, which is equal to the annual budget of the Israeli Ministry of Health in 2008. The study says that because of the burden of the intifada (first and second), the army cannot dissociate himself from political considerations, and finds himself in a conflict and confrontation with politicians and settlers, which leads to the decline of public support for the army, and involves the risk of losing the legitimacy of military service (refusal to service, for example).

Basing on facts and figures, the study goes on to record the burdens of conflict within all fields of state and society, and states that Israel has become internationally subject to condemnation, rejection and boycotts by States and cultural, juridical and academic forums in the West. It is also noted that the conflict resulted in the first assassination in Israel, that of the Prime Minister Yitzhak Rabin in 1995, because of his signing of the Oslo Agreement.

These are three studies, all of which indicate that Israel's future will remain threatened and unaccounted for if its conflict with the Palestinians and the Arabs continues, and if the Zionist approach continues to refuse the withdrawal or refuses to recognize the rights of the Palestinian people. They are all in essence, an appreciation testimony for the Palestinian struggle against the occupation and for the impact of the first and second intifadas on Israel's progress and future.

The urgent need remains for people to read these documents and other documents for a deeper understanding of Israel's reality, for a more accurate vision of its future and for sound decisions in both peace and war. So, is there anyone to read?

Return to the table

THE THIRD PROPHECY

Topographical prophecy occurring before our eyes

Zughar is the name of an ancient water spring located in the south of Tiberias Lake

The dryness of Tiberias Lake, the fruitless of Baisan palm tree and the depletion of the spring of Zughar are considered among the signs predicted by Muhammad, peace be upon him, for the appearance of the Antichrist and the demise of Israel.

The evidence for this comes within the speech of the Prophet (peace be upon him) which was narrated by Fatima Bint Qays (God bless her) regarding the journey of the noble Companion Tamim al-Dari (before he became

Muslim), with some of his friends, when their ship had been tossed by waves in the ocean that took them (near) the land within the ocean (island) and found the Dajjal chained and the below dialogue:

"…Then we hurriedly went on till we came to that monastery and found a well-built person there with his hands tied to his neck and having iron shackles between his two legs up to the ankles. We said:

Woe be upon thee, who are you?

And he said: You would soon come to know about me. But tell me who are you?

We said: We are people from Arabia….

He (that chained person) said: Tell me about the date-palm trees of Baisan.

We said: About what aspect of theirs do you seek information?

He said: I ask you whether these trees bear fruit or not.

Baisan's palm trees; now, they are not bearing fruit.

We said: yes.

Thereupon he said: I think these would not bear fruits.

He said: Inform me about the lake of Tabariyya?

We said: Which aspect of it do you want to know?

He said: Is there water in it?

They said: There is abundance of water in it.

Thereupon he said: I think it would soon become dry.

He again said: Inform me about the spring of Zughar.

They said: Which aspect of it you want to know?

He (the chained person) said: Is there water in it and does it irrigate (the land)?

We said to him: Yes, there is abundance of water in it and the inhabitants (of Medina) irrigate (land) with the help of it…

… I am going to tell you about myself and I am Dajjal…"
[2] Sahih Muslim: 2942 a

The hadith mentioned three things that predict the appearance of the Dajjaal once they occur:

Baisan's fruitless palm trees: Baisan is a Levant country mentioned in the lexicon of countries by Yaqoot Al-Hamawi, mercy be upon him, as he spoke about the palm trees of Baisan and said: "Baisan is a city in Jordan in the Levant valley and it is known to be the tongue of Earth located between Horan and Palestine and has a spring named Al-Falous".

Dryness of Tiberias Lake: this lake is located in the Levant in Palestine, as for the abundance of its water and rivers hundreds of years ago, Yaqoot al-Hamawi said: "Azhari said it is about ten miles in six miles and the lack of its water is a sign for the appearance of the Dajjaal ... As for the lake of Tiberias, I have seen it many times, and it is like a pool Surrounded by the mountains where many rivers coming from the side of Banias, the Coast and the Great Jordan are draining and from which a great river is separated pouring the land of the small Jordan". [4]

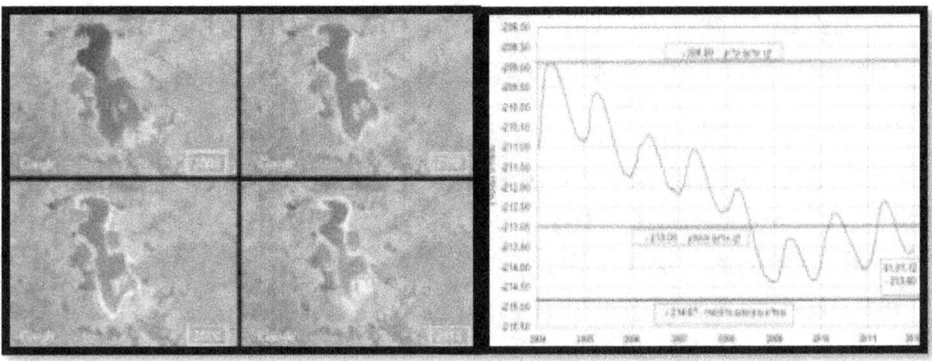

Lack of water level in Tiberias Lake

Now, it is facing a significant shortage in water level, as Isaac Gal from the Supervisory Authority of the lake said: "There is no harm to open a bracket in this section and show even briefly what the Antichrist will be like, because he has a strong relationship with the existence of the Jews as a state in Palestine, as Muhammad (PBUH) told us in Sahih Hadith knowing that his end will bring the end of Jewish military presence in the Holy Land".

An approximate drawing of what the face of Dajjal looks like

First: four consecutive, converging, accelerating, great signs followed by a breakthrough and prosperity and a blessing for safety and security which have never been witnessed before, such as any of the signs of the Great

Hour before the start of major signs of the universe and the sun rises from the opposite 'the west' and others.

The four signs are: the emergence of the Mahdi, the appearance of the Antichrist 'Dajjal', the descent of Jesus 'Isa', the son of Mary, (PBUH), and the coming of Gog and Magog. God willing, I will give these a special edition entitled the Judgement Day's Four Signs.

The signs start in the following order:

1. Emergence of Al-Mahdi **(Mohammad Bin Abdullah):**

A man brought to the right path by Allah in a night and takes allegiance from the Haram al-Makki at the Kaaba, governs between people with fairness and extends his empire over the Peninsula, Khurasana and others. Then there are incidents of evil from Persia, the defeat of an enemy going to Mecca and Medina, a great victory for the Mahdi and his companions and then comes the soldiers of Khorasan, those with black flags, together with the Mahdi do not spare any efforts until they enter Eilat, ie. Beit al-Maqdis (those who carry black flags today like the so-called Islamic State - ISIS - have nothing to do with the matter).

2. Appearance of Dajjal **between Iraq and the Levant:**

A young man with a huge body, a red complexion and long and curly hair, so thick that his locks would look like snakes hanging from his head, lots of them, coiled together; with a prominent forehead and a wide neck. He would be short in height, walk with his feet apart with a hunch in his back. His right eye would be blind like a floating grape, shaking, not fixed in one position and his left eye would be covered with a thick piece of flesh growing at the edge of his eye. He would have the words 'k.f.r' or 'Kafir' written between his eyebrows on his forehead; the literate and illiterate believers of Allah and Islam would clearly be able to see that word, even if others cannot. He would be sterile; he would not have any children. The Dajjal will grow up in a village called Judaism from Isfahaan in Iran, he will Stanford in Kufa and will emerge from the direction of the east between Iraq and the Levant (Syria). Gins and Daemons serve him, he sees angels, he has paranormal powers and magic that cannot be exhibited by other human beings but him. He will reign over all the Middle East, except Mecca and Medina, which he will not be able to enter because the angels are guarding them. His reign and fitnah will last for one and a half year as the Prophet Mohammed (peace be upon him) said. The Mahdi and his companions will be confined to the mountains and the reefs, and they will be then in strain and fitnah that have never been seen since God created Adam until Issah, the son of Mary descend just before dawn.

3. The descent of Issah, (PBUH):

WOULD BE AT THE LIGHTHOUSE IN THE EAST OF DAMASCUS, HIS FACE WOULD GLITTER, AND ON HIS FOREHEAD DROPS WOULD LOOK LIKE PEARLS. THEN HE WOULD ENTER THE UMAYYAD MOSQUE IN DAMASCUS (ACCORDING TO SOME NARRATIONS) AT FAJR PRAYER. HE WOULD BE INVITED TO LEAD THE WORSHIPERS IN PRAYER BUT HE WOULD DENY THAT, AND THEN HE WOULD PRESENT THE MAHDI AHEAD AND PRAYS BEHIND HIM, SO ALL PEOPLE KNOWS THAT HE FOLLOWS ISLAM AND SUBMITS TO ITS LAWS; THEN HE WOULD CALL FOR JIHAD AGAINST THE DAJJAL.

SOME OF THOSE WHO FEARS THE LATTER, SAYS THAT HE IS A JINNI, BUT ISSAH, THE SON OF MARY AND HIS COMPANIONS WOULD GO TO JERUSALEM. ONCE DAJJAL HEARS ABOUT ISSAH AND GETS SURE ABOUT HIM, HE WOULD TRY TO ESCAPE BUT ISSAH WOULD CATCH HIM IN A CITY IN PALESTINE CALLED ALLEDD CITY THEN HE WOULD KILL HIM AND END THE GREATEST FITNAH AND GREATEST DECEIVER IN HISTORY. FOR ME, HE IS MORE LIKELY THE DEVIL 'IBLIS' ITSELF WHO ASKED THE LORD OF THE WORLDS WHEN HE WAS EXPELLED FROM PARADISE, TO SPARE HIM UNTIL THE DAY OF JUDGMENT; WHOM REQUEST WAS ACCEPTED BUT "*TILL THE DAY WHOSE HOUR I KNOW*" (38:81). *"REPRIEVE ME UNTIL THE DAY THEY ARE RESURRECTED. INDEED, YOU ARE OF THOSE REPRIEVED"* AL-ARAF (7:14-15); WE WILL LOOK INTO IT, INCHALLAH, IN A DETAILED VERSION. I SAID THAT ISSAH, PEACE BE UPON HIM AND AL MAHDI WITH HIS COMPANIONS WOULD ENJOY A GREAT VICTORY, JERUSALEM WOULD BE DECLARED AS THE CAPITAL OF MUSLIMS AND ALL MUSLIMS, CHRISTIANS AND JEWS WOULD FOLLOW HIM AND BECOME MUSLIMS AS HE, (PBUH), CALLS FOR THE ISLAM AND HAD BEEN FOLLOWED AND BELIEVED BY THE CHRISTIANS BEFORE, ALTHOUGH HE IS THE SON OF MARY THE VIRGIN, (PUH), WHO IS OF JEWISH ORIGIN. THUS, (PBUH) WOULD COME TO BRING TOGETHER THE PEOPLE OF THE THREE RELIGIONS UNDER THE BANNER OF TAWHEED. HE WOULD UNITE THE NATIONS AND SPREAD THE RELIGION OF MERCY, UNITY, JUSTICE, EQUALITY AND FREEDOM UNTIL GOG AND MAGOG COME OUT.

4. EMERGENCE OF GOG AND MAGOG

IN HUGE NUMBERS FROM THE EAST, I.E., CHINA AND ALL AROUND IT, AND THEY SWIFTLY SWARM FROM EVERY MOUND.

THEY WOULD GO TO JERUSALEM TO KILL ISSAH, (PBUH). THEN THEY WOULD CAMP AROUND THE LAKE TIBERIAS UNTIL THE LAST OF THEM SAYS: THERE WAS ONCE WATER THERE; THEIR CORRUPTION AND INJUSTICE WOULD INCREASE AND THE LORD OF GLORY WILL REVEAL TO ISSAH, SON OF MARY, SPIRIT OF GOD: "I HAVE BROUGHT FORTH FROM AMONGST MY SERVANTS SUCH PEOPLE AGAINST WHOM NONE WOULD BE ABLE TO FIGHT; YOU TAKE THESE PEOPLE SAFELY TO TUR" [NARRATED BY MUSLIM]; I.E. NO ONE HAS THE POWER TO FIGHT THEM.

NARRATED FROM AL-NAWAS IBN SAM'AN, WHO REPORTED IN HIS LONG HADITH "JESUS AND HIS COMPANIONS WOULD THEN BE BESIEGED HERE (AT TUR, AND THEY WOULD BE SO MUCH HARD PRESSED) THAT THE HEAD OF THE OX WOULD BE DEARER TO THEM THAN ONE HUNDRED DINIRS AND ALLAH'S APOSTLE, JESUS, AND HIS COMPANIONS WOULD SUPPLICATE ALLAH, WHO WOULD SEND TO THEM INSECTS (WHICH WOULD ATTACK THEIR NECKS) AND IN THE MORNING THEY WOULD PERISH LIKE ONE SINGLE PERSON. ALLAH'S APOSTLE, JESUS, AND HIS COMPANIONS WOULD THEN COME DOWN TO THE EARTH AND THEY WOULD NOT FIND IN THE EARTH AS MUCH SPACE AS A SINGLE SPAN WHICH IS NOT FILLED WITH THEIR PUTREFACTION AND STENCH. ALLAH'S APOSTLE, JESUS, AND HIS COMPANIONS WOULD THEN AGAIN BESEECH ALLAH, WHO WOULD SEND BIRDS WHOSE NECKS WOULD BE LIKE THOSE OF BACTRIN CAMELS AND THEY WOULD CARRY THEM AND THROW THEM WHERE GOD WOULD WILL. THEN ALLAH WOULD SEND RAIN WHICH NO HOUSE OF CLAY OR (THE TENT OF) CAMELS' HAIRS WOULD KEEP OUT AND IT WOULD WASH AWAY THE EARTH UNTIL IT COULD APPEAR TO BE A MIRROR. THEN THE EARTH WOULD BE TOLD TO BRING FORTH ITS FRUIT AND RESTORE ITS BLESSING AND, AS A RESULT THEREOF, THERE WOULD GROW (SUCH A BIG)

POMEGRANATE THAT A GROUP OF PERSONS WOULD BE ABLE TO EAT THAT, AND SEEK SHELTER UNDER ITS SKIN AND MILCH COW WOULD GIVE SO MUCH MILK THAT A WHOLE PARTY WOULD BE ABLE TO DRINK IT. AND THE MILCH CAMEL WOULD GIVE SUCH (A LARGE QUANTITY OF) MILK THAT THE WHOLE TRIBE WOULD BE ABLE TO DRINK OUT OF THAT AND THE MILCH SHEEP WOULD GIVE SO MUCH MILK THAT THE WHOLE FAMILY WOULD BE ABLE TO DRINK OUT OF THAT" [SAHIH MUSLIM 2937 A]. THEN THE SPIRIT OF GOD, THE SON OF MARY, PBUH, WOULD EXTEND HIS REIGN FORTY YEARS. BEING PROPHETIC, FULL OF PEACE, SAFETY, BLESSING AND MERCY; THEN THAT'S THE END OF HUMANITY THAT BEGAN WITH THE PROPHET ADAM AND ENDS WITH ISSAH SON OF MARY, MAY THE PEACE AND BLESSINGS OF ALLAH BE UPON THEM, BEFORE ALLAH SENDS A PLEASANT WIND TO TAKE THE LIFE OF EVERY BELIEVER AND ONLY THE WICKED WOULD SURVIVE WHO WOULD COMMIT ADULTERY LIKE ASSES UNTIL THE EMERGENCE OF THE BEAST OF THE EARTH AND THE RISING OF THE SUN FROM THE WEST, THEN THE DOOR OF REPENTANCE WOULD CLOSE, THE PENS WOULD BE LIFTED AND THE LAST HOUR WOULD COME TO THEM. ALLAH KNOWS BETTER.

Return to the table

THE FORTH PROPHECY

Henry Kissinger prediction for the demise of Israel in 2022

America's Foreign Minister of Jewish origin expected the demise of Israel in 2022

Kissinger and the prophecy for the end of Israel in 2022: [Monday, 01 October 2012, 06:37]

After his statements about the necessity for the United States of America to occupy seven countries in the Middle

East because of its strategic importance, especially as it contains oil and other economic resources, and there was only one step left on this step which is to bomb Iran. When China and Russia are moving from their snooze to defend their interests in that geographical area of the world then, the "Big Bang" will come and the Great War, where only one force, Israel and America, will be victorious has been occurred and ended. Then, Israel will have to fight with all the strength and weapons it has to kill as many Arabs as possible and occupy half of the Middle East.

Today and again here he comes the former US Secretary of State Henry Kissinger, with a press statement quoted by the New York Post, which is no less surprising than his previous statement delivered to the American newspaper DailyScape, where Kissinger says this time, knowing that he is one of the most prominent veteran political researchers and the American foreign policy's most prominent thinkers and architects for decades, "Ten years later, Israel will no longer exit" and Cindy Adams, the editor of the newspaper said that here article in which she published the statement was accurate, explaining that Kissinger himself had said this sentence which is literally (In 10 years, there will be no more Israel). Therefore, Israel will not be on the international map based on the "Kissinger Prophecy" in 2022.

By going a little bit back, to the time before Kissinger read Israel's horrific tarot, this date, 2021 and 2022, was dealt with in many of the literature of tarot and stars readers and some mythologists, even in Israel itself. Such prophecies can be followed up more on Internet and even many books and volumes have been written on the matter - some of them prestigious and respected ones – such as the book of the Demise of Israel, a Quranic prophecy or a Numerical Coincidence, that was published in 1992 by Bassam JARRAR, a professor of mathematics at Al-Quds University; It was printed in 2000 in Damascus and was published by Dar Al-Shehab, and many more of other books, articles and studies.

❋ ❋ ❋

THE FIFTH PROPHECY

The prophecy of the old Jew and the comet of Halley

Israel's expected life would end with the completion of the Comet Halley's cycle 2022

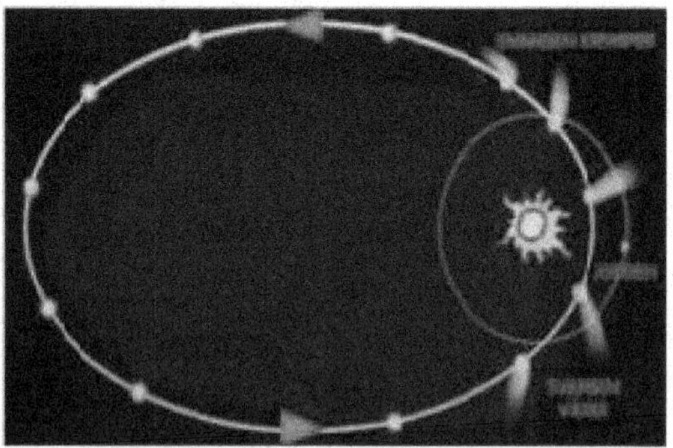

Halley's Comet emerged in the sky in 1948 and will its cycle will be completed in 2022

When the State of Israel was established in 1948, an elderly Iraqi Jew, a neighbor of Dr. Ahmad Al-Rashed,

went to his mother crying, and then she asked her: Why are you crying, while you have a state now?

The Jewish old woman said to her: The establishment of this state will be the reason for slaughtering the Jews. Our prophecy tells us that our country will last for 76 lunar years. "The Jews rely on the lunar calendar like Muslims".

This story reappeared in 1982 during the Israeli invasion of Lebanon where Menachem Begin, a religious political leader, declared at a press conference that Israel would live in peace as stipulated by the Torah for 40 years, and then the Armageddon would be with the Arabs.

Halley's Comet is linked to the beliefs of the Jews, and this comet has two cases: apogee and perigee. Halley's Comet began its astronomical cycle in 1948 at the time of the establishment of the State of Israel.

With regard to Halley's Comet, Al-Khattabi says that the world saw this comet on 10/02/1986 when it was in the apogee phase (the nearest point to the sun), and it was half way to complete its astronomical cycle and the duration was (38) years. If it keeps going with the same speed, then it will complete the cycle in (76) years, which is the age of the State of Israel from its establishment till its demise.

Al-Khattabi also states that the year 1948 corresponded to 1367 in the Hijri calendar, and if we add 1367 AH to 76, The State of Israel's age as in the Jewish prophecy = 1443 Hijri which corresponds 2022 in the Gregorian calendar.

1982, is the year in which Begin said that Israel would enjoy a 40-year peace and if we add it to the invasion year 40+1982 = 2022, which is the demise year as in their prophecy.

Return to the table

THE SIXTH PROPHECY

The demise of Israel, a Quranic prophecy

Why Jerusalem particularly, and the Levant generally are historically and culturally where the rivalry reigns and the nations are dying for them?

The Unitarians spoke their hearts and tongues to mention and pray in occupied Jerusalem

Two surah in the Quran speak with verbosity about the Children of Israel. The first is surat (Yusuf), which tells us the story of the creation of the Children of Israel in detail and in a beautiful and unique narrative style that did not happen with no nation but them. The second surah is (Isra) or also called (Children of Israel). In the beginning of this Surah, the Creator spoke about the journey of the Prophet Muhammad (PBUH) in 621 AD, from Makkah, the Sacred House to Beit al-Maqdis and from there he ascended to heaven, to the presence of God and revealed to him what was revealed, where the Lord established the eternal relationship between the two mosques and the heaven and the basic functions of both mosques.

If the function of the Sacred Mosque is purely spiritual and devotional to the believers of all people, being in harmony with the movement of the universe and its praises;

The function of Jerusalem, in addition to being spiritual, is the confluence of religions and the clash of ideas and wills, and Almighty Allah has made it and what is around it a blessing for the worlds. Knowing that any incident or affliction that affects Jerusalem and the people of the

Levant is for the best and blessing of the worlds sooner or later

The surrender of the crusaders armies before Saladin in Jerusalem on 10/02/1187

Battle of Ain Goliath, End of the Myth of the Mongols:

On the fifth and twentieth of Ramadan in 658 AH, the Muslims won under the leadership of King Muzaffar Seifaldin Qatz in the eternal battle of Ein Ghalout, where the Islamic armies defeated the Tatars, who killed millions of Muslims and others, and defeated the Khilafa of Muslims and its capital Baghdad in 656 AH, corresponding to

September 3, 1260, then Mongols retreated and their dreams about the invasion of the Levant, Turkey and then the Europe fell down.

Napoleon Bonaparte is defeated on the walls of Acre after a long siege in 1799 and gives the order to withdraw. There in the land of Palestine, his dreams of occupying the Levant and the Arabian Peninsula have fell along with his empire successively.

As for the end of Surat "Al-Isra", we have a clear prophecy. It speaks of the permission given to the

Children of Israel to enter the Holy Land and then gather them after their corruption and their end, i.e. the end of their state and their presence in Palestine. Their extermination as claimed by Zionism is not of order, but the Quran predicted that the Muslims would enter the mosque as they entered it the first time without any fighting.

HE ALSO PREDICTED IN ANOTHER VERSE THAT THE JEWS WILL TRY TO RECOVER WHAT THEY LOST AFTER THAT, SAYING: *"IT IS EXPECTED, THAT YOUR LORD WILL HAVE MERCY UPON YOU. BUT IF YOU RETURN, WE WILL RETURN"* [AL-ISRA: 8] BUT NOT A CHANCE.

A LOOK AT SURAT "CHILDREN OF ISRAEL":

A CONFLICT BETWEEN TWO MESSAGES, THE ALMIGHTY SAYS: *"EXALTED IS HE WHO TOOK HIS SERVANT BY NIGHT FROM AL-MASJID AL-HARAM TO AL-MASJID AL- AQSA, WHOSE SURROUNDINGS WE HAVE BLESSED, TO SHOW HIM OF OUR SIGNS. INDEED, HE IS THE HEARING, THE SEEING ❋ AND WE GAVE MOSES THE SCRIPTURE AND MADE IT A GUIDANCE FOR THE CHILDREN OF ISRAEL THAT YOU NOT TAKE OTHER THAN ME AS DISPOSER OF AFFAIRS ❋ O DESCENDANTS OF THOSE WE CARRIED [IN THE SHIP] WITH NOAH. INDEED, HE WAS A GRATEFUL SERVANT"* [AL-ISRA: 1-3], THERE IS ANOTHER NAME OF SURAT AL-ISRA CALLED ALSO CHILDREN OF ISRAEL, IT STARTED BY TELLING ABOUT THE ASCENSION OF THE PROPHET (PBUH) FROM THE SACRED MOSQUE IN MECCA TO THE AL-AQSA MOSQUE IN JERUSALEM AND THEN REFERRED TO THE BLESSING ALLAH MADE IN AL-AQSA MOSQUE AND AROUND IT. THEN IT MOVED DIRECTLY FROM THE ISLAMIC MESSAGE TO THE

MESSAGE OF MOSES, THE PROPHET OF ISRAEL, (PBUH), AND TO THE TORAH, AND WHAT ALLAH MANDATED THE ISRAELITES IN IT.

THE SURAH TOLD US ABOUT THE TWO GREAT SPOILS THAT WERE ASSOCIATED WITH THE GREATNESS AND HAPPENED BY THE JEWS. IT GAVE US THE STATUS OF THE JEWS IN EACH OF THEM, AND DEFINED THE FEATURES OF THE MEN AND THE RABBINIC WORSHIPERS WHO REMOVED THE JEWISH CORRUPTIONS AND IT FOCUSED ON THE SECOND BIG SPOIL OF JEWS. ALLAH WANTS TO DEFINE THE NATURE OF THE CONFLICT WITH THE JEWS, A CONFLICT BETWEEN TWO MESSAGES: THE MESSAGE OF TRUTH, WHICH MUSLIMS REPRESENT AND THE FALSEHOOD MESSAGE REPRESENTED BY THE JEWS WHICH WILL BEGIN ON THE LAND OF THE MEDINA AND ENDS ON THE BLESSED LAND.

HERE IS THE VERSE WHICH IS THE FOCUS OF THE RESEARCH AND PROPHECY:

"AND WE SAID AFTER PHARAOH TO THE CHILDREN OF ISRAEL, DWELL IN THE LAND, AND WHEN THERE COMES THE PROMISE OF THE HEREAFTER, WE WILL BRING YOU FORTH IN GATHERING ✺ AND WITH THE TRUTH WE HAVE SENT THE QUR'AN DOWN, AND WITH THE TRUTH IT HAS DESCENDED AND WE HAVE NOT SENT YOU, EXCEPT AS A BRINGER OF GOOD TIDINGS AND A WARNER". [AL-ISRA: 104-105]

Return to the table

1. IMPORTANT REMARKS ABOUT THE NUMERICAL MIRACLES RELATED TO THIS SUBJECT:

AL-ISRA: NAMED CHILDREN OF ISRAEL, IT MENTIONS TWO OF THEIR SPOILS; THE FIRST WAS ENDED BY NEBUCHADNEZZAR AND THE SECOND IS STILL STANDING ..., AND TWO OF THEIR GLORIFICATIONS; THE FIRST ONE IN THE ERA OF SOLOMON, PEACE BE UPON HIM, WHO WAS A GOOD KING PROPHET. HE FOUNDED A GREAT STATE AND A UNIQUE CIVILIZATION UNTIL HE DIED IN 935 BC. THEN CORRUPTION OCCURRED AFTER HE IS GONE. THE SECOND SPOIL IS UNDOUBTEDLY THE CURRENT ONE.

THE ALMIGHTY SAYS: *"AND WE GAVE MOSES THE SCRIPTURE AND MADE IT A GUIDANCE FOR THE CHILDREN OF ISRAEL THAT YOU NOT TAKE OTHER THAN ME AS DISPOSER OF AFFAIRS* ❀ *...AND WE CONVEYED TO THE CHILDREN OF ISRAEL IN THE SCRIPTURE THAT, "YOU WILL SURELY CAUSE CORRUPTION ON THE EARTH TWICE, AND YOU WILL SURELY REACH [A DEGREE OF] GREAT HAUGHTINESS* ❀ *SO WHEN THE [TIME OF] PROMISE CAME FOR THE FIRST OF THEM...AND WHEN THERE COMES THE PROMISE OF THE HEREAFTER,.."* [AL-ISRA: 2-104].

THE NUMBER OF THE PROPHECY WORDS FROM THE BEGINNING OF *"AND WE GAVE MOSES THE SCRIPTURE"* TILL *"AND WHEN THERE COMES THE PROMISE OF THE HEREAFTER, WE WILL BRING YOU FORTH IN GATHERING"* [AL-ISRA: 104] IS EQUAL TO 1443 WORDS WHICH IS THE SAME NUMBER RESULTING FROM: (1367 AH, THE YEAR OF ISRAEL ESTABLISHMENT + 76, ISRAEL LIFESPAN = 1443).

2. LOOK, WHEN COUNTING FROM THE VERSE 21 OF SURAT AL-MA'IDAH:

ALMIGHTY SAYS: *"O MY PEOPLE, ENTER THE HOLY LAND WHICH ALLAH HAS ASSIGNED TO YOU AND DO NOT TURN BACK [FROM FIGHTING IN ALLAH'S CAUSE] AND [THUS] BECOME LOSERS"* [AL-MAIDA: 21]

START COUNTING FROM THIS VERSE TILL THE VERSE 104 OF AL-ISRA *"AND WHEN THERE COMES THE PROMISE OF THE HEREAFTER, WE WILL BRING YOU FORTH IN GATHERING"* [AL-ISRA: 104]

YOU WILL FIND YOURSELF IN THE VERSE 1443; THE EXPECTED END OF ISRAEL IN HIJIR CALENDAR. SO, IS THIS ALL A COINCIDENCE?

SOLOMON, PEACE BE UPON HIM, DIED IN 935 BC, THE PERIOD BETWEEN THE BEGINNING OF THE FIRST SPOIL AND THE YEAR OF THE ISRA 621 AD IS 1556 YEARS AND THIS IS EQUAL TO THE NUMBER OF WORDS OF SURAT AL-ISRA.

NOTE THAT WHEN SOLOMON DIED IN 935 BC, THE STATE WAS DIVIDED INTO "ISRAEL" IN THE NORTH AND WAS DESTROYED IN 722. THIS YEAR 722 = (38 × 19) BC, AFTER 19 KINGS RULED OVER IT AND ANOTHER ONE CALLED "JUDAH" IN THE SOUTH, WHICH WAS DESTROYED IN 586 BC, 19 KINGS ALSO RULED OVER IT ... SO, IS ISRAEL'S LIFESPAN WILL BE 19 KNESSET?! (19 X 4 = 76).

NOTICE!

SURAT YUSUF SPEAKS ABOUT THE EMERGENCE OF ISRAEL AND THE NUMBER OF ITS VERSES IS 111, SURAT AL ISRA OR CHILDREN OF ISRAEL SPEAKS OF THEIR LAST EXISTENCE IN THE HOLY LAND AND ITS VERSES ARE ALSO 111 KNOWING THAT THERE IS NO OTHER SURAH IN THE HOLY QURAN WITH THE SAME NUMBER OF VERSES WHICH IS 111.

SURAT AL-ISRA ENDS WITH WORDS SUCH AS "وكيلا ... شكورا... نفيرا... لفيفا" IF WE TAKE OUT THE REPEATED WORDS, 76 WORDS REMAIN, WHICH IS THE LIFESPAN OF ISRAEL ($4 \times 19 = 76$).

IN SURAT AL-ISRA WE FIND: THE SEARCH GOES ON...

3. DOES GEMATRIA DETERMINE THE DEMISE DATE OF ISRAEL AND THE ENTRY OF MUSLIMS AS CONQUERORS TO THE MOSQUE OF AL-AQSA?

THE VERSE 104 OF AL-ISRA STATES:

1. *"AND WE SAID AFTER PHARAOH TO THE CHILDREN OF ISRAEL, "DWELL IN THE LAND, AND WHEN THERE COMES THE PROMISE OF THE HEREAFTER, WE WILL BRING YOU FORTH IN [ONE] GATHERING"*. WE HAVE PREVIOUSLY SAID THAT THE ORDER OF THE WORD "لفيفا" *(GATHERING)* WHEN WE START COUNTING FROM THE BEGINNING OF SPEECH IN AL-ISRA PROPHECY IS 1443.

2. THE PHRASE *"AND WHEN THERE COMES THE PROMISE OF THE HEREAFTER"* HAS BEEN REPEATED TWO TIMES WHEN TALKING ABOUT THE END OF THE SECOND SPOIL. IF WE TAKE IN CONSIDERATION THAT THE WORD "الآخرة" (THE HEREAFTER) IS SPELLED ALSO AS "الأخرة", HERE COMES THE

SURPRISE AS THE GEMATRIA OF: *"AND WHEN THERE COMES THE PROMISE OF THE HEREAFTER, WE WILL BRING YOU FORTH IN GATHERING"* IS 2022, SO LOOK CAREFULLY!!

2022, WE SAID THAT THE ORDER OF THE WORD "لفيفا" (GATHERING) IN AL-ISRA'S PROPHECY IS 1443, AND WE SAID THAT THE GEMATRIA OF *"AND WHEN THERE COMES THE PROMISE OF THE HEREAFTER, WE WILL BRING YOU FORTH IN GATHERING"* IS 2022 ACCORDING TO WARSH READING OF THE WORD "الأخرة". HERE, WE ASK WHERE IS THE HEBREW YEAR 5782 THAT CORRESPONDS TO THE YEAR 2022 AD AND 1443 AH?

THE ANSWER

THE ORDER OF THE WORD "لفيفا" IN THE PROPHECY IS 1443, WHICH MEANS THAT THE ORDER OF THE FORTH WORDS COMING AFTER "لفيفا" ARE 1444+1445+1446+1447=5782 AND THOSE WORDS ARE "وبالحق أنزلناه وبالحق نزل..." {*AND WITH THE TRUTH WE HAVE SENT THE QUR'AN DOWN, AND WITH THE TRUTH IT HAS DESCENDED*} [AL-ISRA: 104]. THE SURPRISING HERE IS THE TOTAL OF THESE WORDS ORDER WHICH IS 5782, THE HEBREW DATE THAT CORRESPONDS TO THE YEAR 2022 AD.

NOTICE:

3. THE MOSQUE OF AL-AQSA HAS BEEN DEFINED IN THE HOLY QURAN BY: "الذي باركنا حوله" {*WHOSE SURROUNDINGS WE HAVE BLESSED*} [AL-ISRA: 1] AND THE GEMATRIA OF THIS EXPRESSION ACCORDING TO THE OTTOMAN SCRIPT IS

1063. SO WHAT IS THE WORD WITH THE ORDER OF 1063 IN SURAT AL-ISRA?

a. IT IS THE WORD "يلبثون" {REMAIN}, AND THE DIALECT RELATES TO TIME.

b. IT IS REMARKABLE THAT THIS WORD WAS MENTIONED IN VERSE 76 OF SURAT AL- ISRA.

c. THE GEMATRIA OF THIS WORD IS 598. SO WHAT IF WE ADD IT TO 1063?
$(1063 + 598) = 1661$, THE SURPRISE HERE IS THAT THIS IS THE NUMBER 1443 PLUS THE THE GEMATRIA OF THE WORD "هجري" (HIJIR): = $(1443+218)$.

CONSIDER CAREFULLY!

NOTICE

THE ASSYRIANS OVERTHREW THE STATE OF ISRAEL IN 722 BC, AND THUS ONLY THE STATE OF JUDAH WAS LEFT IN THAT YEAR, WHICH IN TURN LASTED UNTIL 586 BC. WHEN THE STATE OF ISRAEL FELL, THE ORDER OF ITS KING WAS 19 AND HIS NAME WAS (HOSEA). THEN WHEN JUDAH FELL, THE ORDER OF ITS KING WAS ALSO 19 AND HIS NAME (ZEDEKIAH). NOW LET'S CONSIDER THIS SURPRISE:

a. THE GEMATRIA OF (JUDAH) IN ARABIC "يهوذا" IS 722 AND LET'S NOT FORGET THAT IT WAS THE STATE STANDING AFTER THE YEAR 722 BC.

b. WITH THE FALL OF THE STATE OF ISRAEL, THE FIRST SPOIL HAS BEEN PARTIALLY REMOVED AND THE DEMISE HAS BEEN COMPLETED WITH THE FALL OF THE STATE OF JUDA IN 586 BC. THE REMARKABLE HERE IS THAT

THE GEMATRIA OF (HOSEA + ZEDEKIAH) IN ARABIC
"هوشع + صدقيا" IS 586.

OBSERVE CAREFULLY!

Return to the table

THE SEVENTH PROPHECY

The Sabbaths

THE LEVITICUS BOOK, CHAPTER 25 STATES: "THE Lord SAID TO MOSES AT MOUNT SINAI: SPEAK TO THE ISRAELITES AND SAY TO THEM: WHEN YOU ENTER THE LAND I AM GOING TO GIVE YOU, THE LAND ITSELF MUST OBSERVE A SABBATH TO THE Lord. FOR SIX YEARS SOW YOUR FIELDS, AND FOR SIX YEARS PRUNE YOUR VINEYARDS AND GATHER THEIR CROPS. BUT IN THE SEVENTH YEAR THE LAND IS TO HAVE A YEAR OF SABBATH REST, A SABBATH TO THE Lord. DO NOT SOW YOUR FIELDS OR PRUNE YOUR VINEYARDS. DO NOT REAP WHAT GROWS OF ITSELF OR HARVEST THE GRAPES OF YOUR UNTENDED VINES. THE LAND IS TO HAVE A YEAR OF REST". AFTER ELABORATING THE PROVISIONS OF THIS SEVENTH YEAR'S LAW, HE SAYS IN THE CHAPTER 26: "...BUT IF YOU WILL NOT LISTEN TO ME AND CARRY OUT ALL THESE COMMANDS, AND IF YOU REJECT MY DECREES AND ABHOR MY LAWS AND FAIL TO CARRY OUT ALL MY COMMANDS AND SO VIOLATE MY COVENANT, THEN

I WILL DO THIS TO YOU: I WILL BRING ON YOU SUDDEN TERROR…I WILL SCATTER YOU AMONG THE NATIONS AND WILL DRAW OUT MY SWORD AND PURSUE YOU. YOUR LAND WILL BE LAID WASTE, AND YOUR CITIES WILL LIE IN RUINS. 34 THEN THE LAND WILL ENJOY ITS SABBATH YEARS ALL THE TIME THAT IT LIES DESOLATE AND YOU ARE IN THE COUNTRY OF YOUR ENEMIES; THEN THE LAND WILL REST AND ENJOY ITS SABBATHS. 35 ALL THE TIME THAT IT LIES DESOLATE, THE LAND WILL HAVE THE REST IT DID NOT HAVE DURING THE SABBATHS YOU LIVED IN IT…" [1].

THE 2 CHRONICLES BOOK, CHAPTER 36 STATES: "…HE CARRIED INTO EXILE TO BABYLON THE REMNANT, WHO ESCAPED FROM THE SWORD, AND THEY BECAME SERVANTS TO HIM AND HIS SUCCESSORS UNTIL THE KINGDOM OF PERSIA CAME TO POWER. 21 THE LAND ENJOYED ITS SABBATH RESTS; ALL THE TIME OF ITS DESOLATION IT RESTED, UNTIL THE SEVENTY YEARS WERE COMPLETED" [2] AND [3].

THE SABBATH WAS ASSOCIATED WITH THE DEMISE IN JEWISH MEMORY, ESPECIALLY WITH REGARD TO THE HOLY LAND. WE FOUND THAT SOME BELIEVED THAT THE WORLD WOULD DISAPPEAR IN THE HEBREW YEAR 6000, BECAUSE THE SEVENTH MILLENNIUM MEANS DEMISE. IN CONCLUSION, THE SABBATH IS RELATED TO THE NUMBER (7). IT IS CLEAR IN THE HOLY QURAN THAT THE LAW OF THE SABBATH HAS A PRESENCE IN THE RELIGION OF MOSES, PEACE BE UPON HIM, REGARDLESS OF THE DETAILS, AND IT IS INTERESTING TO NOTE THAT THE WORD "السبت" [AL-BAQARAH: 65] HAS BEEN REPEATED IN THE HOLY QURAN (5) TIMES AND IF THE TWO WORDS "سبتهم ويسبتون", THE TOTAL IS 7 TIMES. ALSO, THE FACT THAT 3 OF THEM I.E.: "السبت وسبتهم ويسبتون" ARE

STATED IN SURAT AL-ARAF WHICH ORDER IN THE QURAN IS 7 DRAWS ATTENTION!. IN ADDITION TO THE FACT THAT THE LAST TIME THE WORD السبت (SABBATH) HAS BEEN MENTIONED IN THE HOLY QURAN IS IN THE VERSE 124 OF SURAT AL-NAHL, I.E. IN THE LAST VERSES OF THE SURAH THAT PRECEDES.

SABBATHS IN HISTORY:

EVERY SABBATHS IS 7 YEARS LONG. SO, HOW MANY DAYS THE SOLAR YEAR EXCEED THE LUNAR? INTERESTINGLY, IT EXCEEDS BY 76 DAYS. THIS REMINDS US OF THE NUMBER 76 IN SURAT AL-ISRA, IN PARTICULAR VERSE 76, WHICH SPEAKS OF EVICTING. BUT THE VERSE 77 STATES THAT WHAT IS MENTIONED IN VERSE 76 IS AN ESTABLISHED WAY IN THE PAST AND THE FUTURE.

THE NUMBER OF WORDS IS THE LATTER VERSE IS 11, WHICH IS REMARKABLE AS WHEN WE PROCEED WITH $(77 \div 7) = 7$. WE NOTICE THAT THE NUMBER OF WORDS FROM VERSE (124) OF SURAT AN-NAHL, WHICH IS THE LAST VERSE IN THE QURAN'S ORDER WHERE THE SABBATH IS MENTIONED, AND EVEN THE VERSE FROM SURAT AL-ISRA: *"AND WE GAVE MOSES THE SCRIPTURE..."* IS ALSO (77) WORDS.

WE CONSIDERED TAKING THE NUMBER 7 AS A MATHEMATICAL UNIT, AND THEN WE FOUND THAT THIS NUMBER IS RELATED TO THE HISTORY OF THE HOLY LAND. IT IS AMAZING THAT ALL OF THIS IS RELATED TO THE GEMATRIA OF THE FOLLOWING WORDS AND PHRASES: (AL-MASJID AL-HARAM, AL-AQSA MOSQUE, BANI ISRAEL, BANU ISRAEL, ISRAEL, SABBATH, ISRA). SOME OF THESE WORDS' SPELLING DIFFERS FROM THE WRITING ACCORDING TO THE OTTOMAN SCRIPT. FOR INSTANCE, THE WORD (إسرائيل) IS WRITTEN IN THE

QURAN (إسرءيل) WHICH IMPLICATES A DIFFERENCE IN ITS NUMERICAL VALUE. FINALLY, IT IS NOTEWORTHY THAT THE NUMBER OF SABBATHS IN 13 YEARS, FOR EXAMPLE, IS ONE SABBATH, AS IN THE 7 YEARS, UNTIL THE COMPLETION OF 14 YEARS AND SO ON...

THE NUMERICAL VALUE OF THE EXPRESSION (بني إسرءيل) ACCORDING TO GEMATRIA IS 365, WHICH IS THE NUMBER OF DAYS OF THE SOLAR YEAR. BUT ACCORDING TO THE OTTOMAN SCRIPT, THE LETTER (ألف) IS MISSING LIKE THIS: (بني إسرءيل) AND THEN THE NUMERICAL VALUE BECOMES (364). THE NUMERICAL VALUE OF THE EXPRESSION (بنو إسرءيل) IS (361).

THIS VALUE DOES NOT DIFFER IN QURAN SCRIPT, BECAUSE THE MISSING LETTER IN THE WORD (إسرءيل) IS ADDED TO THE WORD (بنوا) AND THEN THE EXPRESSION IS WRITTEN AS FOLLOW: (بنوا إسرءيل). THUS, THE TOTAL WOULD BE (361) WHICH IS (19x19). AGAIN, WHAT IS IMPRESSIVE HERE IS THAT THE NUMERICAL VALUE OF THE EXPRESSION (المسجد الأقصا) ACCORDING TO OTTOMAN SCRIPT IS (361) NOTING THAT THE AL-AQSA MOSQUE HAS BEEN STATED IN QURAN JUST ONCE IN SURAT AL-ISRA WHICH IS NAMED ALSO CHILDREN OF ISRAEL (بني إسرائيل) AND WITHOUT ADDITION (بنو إسرءيل)!!

THE NUMERICAL VALUE OF THE WORD (إسرءيل) ACCORDING TO THE OTTOMAN SCRIPT IS (302), WHILE THAT OF THE WORD (السبت) IS (493). FOR THE EXPRESSION (المسجد الحرام), THE NUMERICAL VALUE IS (418) WHICH IS (22x19). THEREFORE, THE TOTAL OF THE GEMATRIA OF: (المسجد الأقصا) + (المسجد الحرام) IS (779) IE. (41x19).

THE FIRST COMPLETE DEMISE WAS IN 586 BC [5], AS JERUSALEM WAS ENTERED AND THE TEMPLE WAS DESTROYED, AS STATED

BEFORE. FOR THE SECOND DEMISE, AS AFOREMENTIONED, IT WAS IN TWO PHASES: THE FIRST PHASE IN 1948 AND THE SECOND STAGE BY ENTERING JERUSALEM IN 1967. WE HAVE ALREADY POINTED OUT THAT THE PARTIAL ESTABLISHMENT OF ISRAEL WAS IN 10/06/1948 AD, THE DATE OF THE FIRST TRUCE. THE TRUCE OF 1967 WAS ALSO ON 10/06. IF WE KNOW THAT THE DESTRUCTION OF THE FIRST TEMPLE AND THE SECOND TEMPLE WAS ON AUGUST 8, 586 BC, WE REALIZED THAT THE DATE (10/06) IN THE YEARS (1948, 1967) MAKES ANY SUM OF THE YEARS OF (586 BC - 1948 AD) AND (586 BC - 1967 AD) IS LESS THAN TWO COMPLETE MONTHS. THEREFORE, WE FIND OUT THAT THE NUMBER OF SABBATHS BETWEEN (586 BC – 1948 AD) IS 361, WHICH IS THE GEMATRIA OF (بنو إسرءيل) AND THAT OF (المسجد الأقصا) ACCORDING TO QURAN SCRIPT, AND THAT THE NUMBER OF THE SABBATHS BETWEEN (586 BC - 1967 AD) IS (364) WHICH IS THE GEMATRIA OF (بني إسرءيل) ACCORDING TO QURAN SCRIPT. AFTER THE ENTRY OF JEWS TO JERUSALEM, THE SABBATH WAS THE NUMBER (365) WHICH IS THE GEMATRIA OF (بني إسرءيل) ACCORDING TO THE WORD, THUS COMPLETING AN ASTRONOMICAL CYCLE [7].

THE ASSYRIANS DESTROYED THE KINGDOM OF ISRAEL IN 722 BC, AND THE CHALDEANS DESTROYED THE KINGDOM OF JUDAH IN 586 BC. THIS MEANS THAT THE KINGDOM OF JUDAH EXTENDED MORE THAN 136 YEARS WHICH INCLUDED (19) SABBATHS.

LANGUAGE IS A HUMAN IDIOM. [8] THE MESSAGES HAVE BEEN REVEALED IN THE LANGUAGES OF DIFFERENT PEOPLES AND THE HISTORY WITH EITHER AH. OR AD. IS ALSO AN IDIOM; IF, FOR EXAMPLE, IT IS SAID THAT THIS YEAR IS 1993 AFTER THE BIRTH OF CHRIST, THIS DOES NOT MEAN THAT WE ARE CERTAIN THAT JESUS, PEACE BE UPON HIM, WAS BORN BEFORE 1993 YEARS AGO, BUT WE GOT USED THE THIS TERM, WHICH CAN BE REALISTIC, OR MAY NOT.

NEVERTHELESS, OUR AGREEMENT ON THIS DATE MAKES IT AUTHENTIC AND CORRECT, SAME AS THE LANGUAGE.

IN THE BOOK "ALLAH, PROPHETS IN THE TORAH AND THE OLD TESTAMENT" STATES: (...DR. MAURICE BUCAILLE CONCLUDED BY SAYING THAT THE BANISHMENT OF PHARAOH WAS "MANBATTAH" THE SON OF RAMSES II. SINCE MANBATTAH TOOK OVER THE THRONE OF EGYPT IN 1224 BC, FOR TEN YEARS IN ONE STATEMENT, AND TWENTY YEARS IN ANOTHER, THE YEAR OF BANISHMENT IS EITHER (1214 BC.) OR (1204 BC.)[9]. IN THE LIGHT OF WHAT PRECEDED HERE COME THESE OBSERVATIONS:

1204 BC. Banishment from Egypt [10]
935 BC. Death of Solomon, peace be upon him.
722 BC. Destruction of the north state of Israel
586 BC. Destruction of the south state of Judah

1948 AD., 1967 AD. and 2022 AD. are years of: establishment of Israel, Entry to Al-Quds and the likely expected Demise. With regard to the aforementioned, it is impressive to note that:

a. **The number of Hebrew years before 1204 BC equals 365 Sabbaths, which is equal to one astronomical cycle of the earth around the sun.**
b. **There is 38 Sabbaths from the year 1204 BC till the year 935 BC, ie. (2×19).**
c. **There is (19) Sabbaths from the demise of the First State in 722 BC till the demise of the Second State in 586 BC.**
d. **There is 361 Sabbaths from the first demise in 586 BC till the second establishment in 1948 AD. ie. (19x19) [11]**

e. There is 364 Sabbaths from the banishment in 586 BC till the return in 1967 AD, which is the Gematria of (بني إسرءيل) according to Quran script.

f. The Sabbaths number (365) occurs after entering Al-Quds, thus completing one astronomical cycle of the Sabbath, which is the same number for Sabbaths before the date of banishment from Egypt, as stated in point (a.) which is the Gematria of (بني إسرءيل) according to the spelling.

g. Number of Sabbaths from the death of Solomon, peace be upon him, in 935 BC to the expected demise in 2022 is (422). The Sabbaths from the beginning of Hebrew history until the date of the death of Solomon, peace be upon him, is (403). Therefore, the difference is 19 Sabbaths.

h. Number of Sabbaths from the death of Solomon, peace be upon him, in 935 BC to 2022 AD is 422. Then what is this number?!

If we gather the order of Surat Al-Isra, the number of its verses and the Gematria of its name, the result is: (17+294+111) = 422 then observe carefully!

i. The year 2022 AD corresponds the Hebrew year of 5782. We have found that the number of Sabbaths till this year is: (5782 ÷ 7) = 826. It is recognized that the Sabbaths implicates interruption, and the surprising here is that the Gematria of (سبت بني إسرءيل) is also 826.

In 1969 AD, an astronomical cycle of Sabbaths has been completed, ie. (365) Sabbaths starting from the demise of the first state till the banishment from Jerusalem. This year coincides with the Hebrew year (5730) which presents remarkably the half-life of carbon 14 [12], used by archaeologists to determine the age of humanity and human civilization. This year is positioned in the cycle 302 of the number 19 [13] and the number (302) is the Gematria of the word (إسرءيل) according to the Ottoman script. This means that the State of Israel occupied Jerusalem in the Israel round of the number 19.

j. The value of the word AD (ميلادي) in Gematria is (95). Therefore: (2022 + 95) = 2117 AD, and in this number (302) Sabbaths. Does this indicate the Sabbath of Israel, ie. its demise?! Let's not forget that the last time the word (السبت) is mentioned is in the last verses of Surat Al-Nahl, which comes in the order of the Koran before Surat Al-Isra.

k. We said before that every seven years includes one Sabbath, and we have been impressed by the fact that the Gematria of the expression (سبع سنين) corresponds to 302, which is that of (إسرءيل). Then observe carefully!!

The number of year from 935 BC to 621 AD is 1556 solar years. The number of the solar years from 621 AD to 2022 AD, as already shown, is 1400.4 solar years. Therefore, the difference is 155.6 solar years, which we have demonstrated before to be the 1/19 of the total both periods. If we deduct 155.6 years from

935 BC, then we will be in the year 779 BC which is characterized by the following:

a. **779 is (19x41)**
b. **57 years after 779 BC, the first Israel demised, ie. in 722 BC. 57 years after 1967 AD [14] the second Israel is expected to demise [15] and if we multiply 722 by 2, the result will be: (722x2) = 1444, which is impressively the 19th multiple of the expected lifespan of Israel; ie. 76 which is also the number of lunar years from 621 AD to 2022 AD.**

THE GEMATRIA OF (المسجد الأقصا) IS 361 AND THAT OF (المسجد الحرام) IS 418. THE DIFFERENCE BETWEEN THE TWO GEMATRIAS IS (57) AND THE TOTAL IS: (361+418) = 779 WHICH IS (41 x 19). THE IMPRESSIVE HERE IS THAT (41) IS THE GEMATRIA OF (إلى). NOW, LET'S CONSIDER THE POSITION OF THE LATTER IN THE FIRST VERSE OF SURAT AL-ISRA: *"EXALTED IS HE WHO TOOK HIS SERVANT BY NIGHT FROM AL-MASJID AL-HARAM TO AL-MASJID AL-AQSA..."*

EXTRACTED FROM THE NOON CENTER FOR QURANIC STUDIES AND OTHERS.

<u>RETURN TO THE TABLE</u>

THE EIGTH PROPHECY

Does Israel demise on 08/07/2022, corresponding to 09 /12/1443 the day of arafa?

DR. BASSAM JARRAR, DIRECTOR OF NOON CENTER FOR QURANIC STUDIES

DR. BASSAM JARRAR, A PROFESSOR OF MATHEMATICS, DID NOT ONLY PREDICT THE DEMISE OF ISRAEL IN 2022, CORRESPONDING TO 1443 AH, AND TO 5782 IN HEBREW, IN A SMART, CONVINCING AND REASONABLE ALGORITHM, HE DID EVEN DEFINED THE DATE BY THE DAY, NAMES, AND SOME OF WHAT I LEARNED AND VERIFIED, THE DETAILS ARE AS FOLLOW:

BEFORE THAT, I WOULD LIKE TO REMIND THE READER TO RECONSIDER THE CALCULATION OF GEMATRIA WE HAVE MENTIONED BEFORE.

جدول حساب الجمّل

400 ت	60 س	8 ح	1 ا
500 ث	70 خ	9 ط	2 ب
600 خ	80 ف	10 ي	3 ج
700 ذ	90 ص	20 ك	4 د
800 ض	100 ق	30 ل	5 ه
900 ظ	200 ر	40 م	6 و
1000 غ	300 ش	50 ن	7 ز

THE NUMERICAL VALUE OF THE ARABIC ALPHABET

KEY WORD

BALANCE (الميزان) 456

A mathematical equation discovered from the verse 25 of Surat Al-Hadid: "We have already sent Our messengers with clear evidences and sent down with them the Scripture and the balance that the people may maintain in justice"[Al-Hadid: 25]. The number of the word in the surah is 456 and its usefulness is illustrated in the following example:

1. IF YOU CALCULATE:
   AH هجري 218 + 1443) – (ميلادي GEMATRIA OF) 95 + 2022
   (= 456 الميزان)

2. IF YOU CALCULATE:
   اربع مائة GEMATRIA OF 1548) + 456 + 2022 + 95 + 218 + 1443
   وست وخمسون) = 5782

   THE EXPECTED RESULT IS THE HEBREW DATE IN 2022 AD.

3. IF YOU CALCULATE:
   = (1443+) للهجرة 273) + (2022 + للميلاد 144)+ 456 + 1548
   5886

   2022 + 1443 + 1187 + 583 + 636 + 15 = 5886

   THE EXPECTED RESULT IS THE THREE CONQUESTS IN AD AND AH

   Next conquest (2022 + 1443) + Salahuddin's conquest (1187 + 583)   + Omar's conquest (636 + 15) in AD and AH=5886

THE NUMERICAL VALUE OF THE KEY WORDS:

361 = GEMATRIA OF MASJID AL-AQSA (المسجد الأقصى)

205 = GEMATRIA OF RAJAB (رجب)

218 = GEMATRIA OF HIJIR (هجري)

1443 AH CORRESPONDING TO 2022 AD/ BEIT AL-MAQDIS' CONQUEST

273 = FOR THE HIJIR (للهجرة)

1808 : 1443 : GEMATRIA

1548 : 456 : GEMATRIA

27/07/583 SALAHUDDIN AL-AYYUBI'S CONQUEST FOR THE HIJIR

EXPECTED CONQUEST OF BEIT AL-MAQDIS 2022 AD CORRESPONDING TO 1443 AH.

OMAR IBN AL-KHATTAB'S CONQUEST OF JERUSALEM WAS IN 15 AH.

GEMATRIA OF THE WORD CONQUEST (فتح) = 488

GEMATRIA OF MILADI (ميلادي) = 95

GEMATRIA OF TWO THOUSAND AND TWENTY TWO (ألفان واثنين وعشرون) = 1401

GEMATRIA OF BALANCE (الميزان) = 456

"SO BE NOT IMPATIENT OVER THEM. WE ONLY COUNT OUT TO THEM A [LIMITED] NUMBER" [MARIAM: 84]

GEMATRIA OF THE BLESSED LAND (الأرض المباركة) = 1818

GEMATRIA OF WEDNESDAY (الأربعاء) = 306

ALMIGHTY SAYS: *"...SO FEAR THEM NOT BUT FEAR ME..."* [AL-BAQARAH: 150]

GEMATRIA OF DAY OF ARAFA (يوم عرفة) = 411

GEMATRIA OF DHUL-HIJJA (ذو الحجة) = 753

GEMATRIA OF AL-ARAF (الأعراف) = 383

GEMATRIA OF THE VERSE *"[THEIR] ASSEMBLY WILL BE DEFEATED, AND THEY WILL TURN THEIR BACKS [IN RETREAT]"* (سيهزم الجمع ويولون الدبر) [AL-QAMAR: 45] = 611

GEMATRIA OF FOR THE AD (للميلادي) = 144

GEMATRIA OF FOR THE AH (للهجري) = 273

GEMATRIA OF THEIR SABBATH (سبتهم) = 528

GEMATRIA OF SABBATH (السبت) = 493

GEMATRIA OF (يسبتون) = 507

GEMATRIA OF WEDNESDAY (الأربعاء) = 306

THE BLESSED LAND CONQUEST:

DHUL-HIJJA (ذو الحجة) = 753

1443 IN ARABIC LETTERS (ألف وأربع مائة وثلاث وأربعون) = 1808

PALESTINE (فلسطين) = 239

"[THEIR] ASSEMBLY WILL BE DEFEATED, AND THEY WILL TURN THEIR BACKS [IN RETREAT]" (سيهزم الجمع ويولون الدبر) [AL-QAMAR: 45]

"THE SABBATH WAS ONLY APPOINTED FOR THOSE WHO DIFFERED OVER IT" [AL-NAHL: 124] = 2802

AD (ميلادي) = 95

FIELD OF SEARCH

HAVİNG CONSİDERED THE SEARCH TOOLS AND GAVE NUMERİCAL VALUE SUBJECT TO THE GEMATRİA RULE, THE NUMERİCAL RESEARCH WİLL FOCUS ON THREE ASPECTS ONLY. WE WİLL BE LİMİTED TO THİS SO THAT THE SUBJECT WON'T GET COMPLİCATED.

1. FİRST SEARCH

IT DEALS WİTH THE SABBATH İN THE QURAN AS THE SABBATH İS CONSİDERED A LAW AMONG THE JEWS, AND İT MEANS İNTERRUPTİON. IT İS ALSO MENTİONED İN THE QURAN SEVEN TİMES AS WE HAVE DEMONSTRATED BEFORE; IF THAT İMPLİCATES CONNOTATİONS?

2. SECOND NUMERİCAL SEARCH

ADDRESSES THE CONVERGENCE OF THE DAY OF MUSLİMS (AL-AİD), DAY OF ARAFA AND THE DAY OF JEWS ON DAY OF ATONMENT OR YOM KİPPUR ON 23/09/2015 İF THAT WAS A SECRET, A RELATİONSHİP OR A DİVİNE SİGN FOR THE END OF ISRAEL EXPECTED İN 2022?

3. THİRD AND FİNAL SEARCH

ADDRESSES THE LAST VERSE WHERE THE SABBATH İS MENTİONED İN THE QURAN, VERSE 124 OF SURAT AL-NAHL, WHİCH CAME FOUR VERSES BEFORE THE BEGİNNİNG OF SURAT CHİLDREN OF ISRAEL (AL-ISRA), İN WHİCH THE GATHERİNG OF JEWS AND THEİR END WAS MENTİONED. IF THAT WAS A SİGN?

SEARCH İN SABBATHS, AL-ARAF 163:

"AND ASK THEM ABOUT THE TOWN THAT WAS BY THE SEA - WHEN THEY TRANSGRESSED IN [THE MATTER OF] THE SABBATH - WHEN THEIR FISH CAME TO THEM OPENLY ON THEIR SABBATH DAY, AND THE DAY THEY HAD NO SABBATH THEY DID NOT COME TO THEM. THUS DID WE GIVE THEM TRIAL BECAUSE THEY WERE DEFIANTLY DISOBEDIENT" [AL-ARAF: 163].

GEMATRIA:

3500 = (السبت) 2465 = (5 x 493) + (سبتهم) 528 + (يسبتون) 507

GEMATRIA OF THE EXPECTED RESULT = GEMATRIA OF 1818 + 1443 + 236:

GEMATRIA OF 3500 = 1443 AH + PALESTINE (فلسطين) + BLESSED LAND CONQUEST (فتح الأرض المباركة)

ADJUSTMENT BY BALANCE (تعديل الميزان):

(1548 + 456) – 3500 = 1496

NOTICE ALSO, 1496 = 95 + 1401 WHICH IS THE GEMATRIA OF 2022 AD IN ARABIC LETTERS (ميلادي)

1443 IS ALSO EQUAL TO THE NUMBER OF YEARS FROM AL-ISRA DATE 621 AD TO THE YEAR 2022 AD; THE HIJIR IS 1401G.

YEARS FROM THE DATE OF AL-ISRA (س من تاريخ الإسراء) 1444 = 19 x 76 = 1 + YEAR (سنة)

THIS IS ALSO THE EXPECTED RESULT:

1135 BEIT AL-MAQDIS CONQUEST (فتح بيت المقدس) + 361 MASJID AL-AQSA (مسجد الأقصا) = 1496

ORDER OF THE VERSE 163 OF AL-ARAF FROM THE BEGINNING OF THE QURAN IS 1117

(ترتيب الآية 163 من سورة الأعراف من بداية المصحف)

$1117 + 163 + (383)$ AL-ARAF (الأعراف) $= 1663$

EXPECTED RESULT = MASJID AL-AQSA (مسجد الأقصى) + "الذي باركنا حوله"

{WHOSE SURROUNDINGS WE HAVE BLESSED} + PALESTINE (فلسطين)

$G. \ 1663 = G. + 1063G + 239 + 361 =$

ORDER OF THE VERSE 163 OF AL-ARAF FROM THE END OF THE QURAN $= 5120$

(ترتيب الآية 163 من الأعراف من نهاية المصحف)

THE ORDER OF THE VERSE IN THE SURAH (ترتيب الآية في السورة) + FROM THE END OF THE QURAN (من نهاية المصحف) $= 5120 + 163 = 5283$

EXPECTED RESULT:

$1443 + 2022 + (1818)$ BLESSED LAND CONQUEST (فتح الأرض المباركة) $= 5283$

SEARCH:

TOTAL NUMBER OF VERSES WHERE THE WORD SABBATH HAS BEEN MENTIONED IS:

$124 + 163 + 154 + 47 + 65 = 553$

$553 + 2456 = 5 \times (493)$ SABBATH $= 3018$

EXPECTED RESULT:

273 + 1443 + (239 + 1063) (PALESTINE + *WHOSE SURROUNDINGS WE HAVE BLESSED*) = 1302 FOR HIJIR (الهجرة)

THIS IS ALSO: *"VICTORY FROM ALLAH AND AN IMMINENT CONQUEST"* [AL-SAF: 13] = 3018

SEARCH İN AL-NAHL VERSE 124:

"THE SABBATH WAS ONLY APPOINTED FOR THOSE WHO DIFFERED OVER IT. AND INDEED, YOUR LORD WILL JUDGE BETWEEN THEM ON THE DAY OF RESURRECTION CONCERNING THAT OVER WHICH THEY USED TO DIFFER" [AL-NAHL: 124].

GEMATRIA: (إنما جعل السبت على الذين اختلفوا فيه) *"THE SABBATH WAS ONLY APPOINTED FOR THOSE WHO DIFFERED OVER IT"*

EXPECTED RESULT = 2802

CONQUEST (488) + 15 + 583 + 1443 + الهجرة 273 = 2802

FULL VERSE: *"THE SABBATH WAS … THEY USED TO DIFFER"* = 5018

EXPECTED RESULT: = 2802

5018 = 361 + 1135 + 1401 + 95 + 1808 + 218

BEIT AL-MAQDIS CONQUEST + MASJID AL-AQSA + 1443 + AH + 2022 + AD = 5018

SEARCH İN VERSE 124 COMPLETE MİSSİNG İTS BEGİNNİNG:

$5018 - 2802 = 2216$

Integration of the balance (الميزان) $= 2216 - 456 = 1760$

Expected result:

Holy Land conquest

(Balance $456 + 1548$) $+ 2216 = 4220$ or

Expected result: $15 + 361 + 1818 + 583 + 1443 = 4220$

Salahuddin's conquest $583 + 15$ Omar's conquest $+ 361$ masjid Al-Aqsa $+ 1818$ Blessed Land conquest $= 1443$ next conquest

It is also: $1135 + 1063 + 2022 =$

$2022 + 1063$ *whose surroundings we have blessed* $+$ Beit Al-Maqdis conquest $= 4220$

It is also:

$273 + 144 + 583 + 7 + 27 + 1760$ (Holy Land Conquest) $+ 239$ (Palestine) $+ 1187 = 4220$

Expected result:

Holy Land Conquest

For AD $(144) + 1187 + (273)$ for Hijri $27/07/583 + (239)$ Palestine $+ (1760) = 4220$

Second Search:

CONVERGENCE OF THE DAY OF ARAFA, DAY OF GREAT HAJJ **AND**
ATONEMENT **DAY**, THE BEST DAY FOR JEWS

THE NATIONS OF SHOULDER TO SHOULDER JEWS FAST THE
DAY OF ATONEMENT
          FASTS THE DAY OF ARAFA

ONE OF THE AMAZING COMPROMISES OF THE YEAR 2015 IS THE
CONVERGENCE OF THE MOST IMPORTANT DAY OF MUSLIMS, ON
THE SAME DAY, AND THE MOST IMPORTANT DAY OF JEWS ON
YOM KIPPUR, WEDNESDAY 23/09/2015 AD CORRESPONDING
TO 09/12/1436 AH. SO, DOES THIS IMPLICATE ANY SIGNS?

NOTICE THE HIJIR DATE: 9 DHUL-HIJJA 753 + 218 AH + 1436
(HIJIR YEAR) = 2416

EXPECTED RESULT:

IT IS THE GEMATRIA OF *"INDEED, IT IS WE WHO SENT DOWN THE
QUR'AN AND INDEED, WE WILL BE ITS GUARDIAN"* [AL-HIJR: 9] =
2416

THE WORD GUARDİAN (الحافظون) İS WRİTTEN İN OTTOMAN SCRİPT WİTHOUT THE ALPHABET 'ALİF' (لحفظون)

EXPECTED RESULT:

239 PALESTİNE + 1063 *WHOSE SURROUNDİNGS WE HAVE BLESSED* + MASJİD AL-AQSA 361 + 753 + DHUL-HİJJA = 2416

NOTICE THE AD DATE:

2015 (ميلادي) (AD) + 95 + 23 SEPTEMBER (أيلول) + 77 = 2210

GEMATRIA OF *"WE HAVE ALREADY SENT OUR MESSENGERS WITH CLEAR EVIDENCES AND SENT DOWN WITH THEM THE SCRIPTURE AND THE BALANCE…"* [AL-HADID: 25] = 2210

SUM THE GEMATRIA OF BOTH AD AND AH DATES OF THE CONVERGENCE DAY

2210 + 2416 = 4626

(1548 + BALANCE 456) − 4626 = 2622

EXPECTED RESULT:

(239) PALESTINE + (361) MASJİD AL-AQSA + 2022 = 2622

NOTICE WHEN ADDRESSED BY THE BALANCE:

2210 − 2416 = 206

2210 = (1548 + 456) + 206 TO RETURN TO ITS FIRST VALUE.

NOTICE WHEN SUMMING BOTH DATES:

2015 + 23 + SEPTEMBER 77 + 1436 + DHUL-HIJJA 9 = 4313

EXPECTED RESULT:

HOLY LAND CONQUEST 1760 + PALESTINE 239 + OMAR'S CONQUEST 15 + SALAHUDDIN'S CONQUEST 583 + NEXT CONQUEST 1443 + FOR HIJIR 273 = 4313

NOTICE:

9 DHUL-HIJJA + 753 + 1436 + FOR HIJIR 273 + 23 + SEPTEMBER 77 + 2015 + FOR AD 144 = 4730

EXPECTED RESULT:

HOLY LAND 1760 + GEMATRIA OF 2022 IN ARABIC LETTERS (1401) + PALESTINE 239 + BLESSED LAND 1330 = 4730

IT IS ALSO:

DHUL-HIJJA + MASJID AL-AQSA + *WHOSE SURROUNDINGS WE HAVE BLESSED* + PALESTINE + OMAR'S CONQUEST + SALAHUDDIN'S CONQUEST + NEXT CONQUEST + FOR HIJIR = 4730

583 + 15 + (PALESTINE) 239 + (*WHOSE SURROUNDINGS WE HAVE BLESSED*) 1063 + (MASJID AL-AQSA) 361 + (DHUL-HIJJA) 753 + (FOR HIJIR) 273 + 1443 = 4730

IT IS ALSO:

1443 + (SALAHUDDIN'S CONQUEST) 583 + (OMER'S CONQUEST) 15 + (*INDEED, IT IS WE WHO SENT DOWN THE QUR'AN AND INDEED, WE WILL BE ITS GUARDIAN*) [AL-HIJR: 9] 2416 + FOR HIJIR 273 + (NEXT CONQUEST) = 4730

NOTICE:

9 DHUL-HIJJA 753 = 762 = WEDNESDAY 306 + 456 = 762

NOTICE:

HIJIR 1436 + (753) 9 DHUL-HIJJA = 2198

EXPECTED RESULT:

(1135) BEIT AL-MAQDIS' CONQUEST + *WHOSE SURROUNDINGS WE HAVE BLESSED* 1063 = 2298

INTEGRATING BALANCE:

2198 - 1548 = 650

EXPECTED RESULT:

(DAY OF ARAFA) 411 + (PALESTINE) 239 = 650

OBSERVE CAREFULLY!

(FOR HIJIR) 273 + 1436 + (753) HIJJA (9) DHUL = 2471

AD DATE CORRESPONDING TO THE YEAR 1436 IS 2471 − 456 = 2015

SUM OF BOTH HIJIR AND AD DATES:

23/09/2015 + 09/12/1436 = 3504

ADDRESSING IT BY BALANCE:

3504 − 1548 = 1956

EXPECTED RESULT:

(FOR AD) 144 + TWO THOUSAND TWENTY TWO + (411) DAY OF ARAFA = 1956

NOTICE!

(GEMATRIA OF 2022) 1401 + (2416… *"INDEED, IT IS WE WHO SENT DOWN THE QUR'AN AND INDEED, WE WILL BE ITS GUARDIAN"*) = 3817

OBSERVE CAREFULLY!

95 **AD** + 23/09/2015 + 218 **AH** + 09/12/1436 = 3817

EXPECTED RESULT:

"INDEED, IT IS WE WHO SENT DOWN THE QUR'AN AND INDEED, WE WILL BE ITS GUARDIAN" **2416** − 3817 = 1401 GEMATRIA OF TWO THOUSAND TWENTY TWO

OBSERVE CAREFULLY!

(144) FOR AD + 23/09/2015 + 09/12/1436 + (273) FOR HİJİR = 3921

OBSERVE CAREFULLY!

3465 = BALANCE 456 − **3921**

EXPECTED RESULT:

3465 = 1443 + 2022 VERY İMPRESSİVE!

NOTİCE WHEN İNTEGRATİNG WEDNESDAY

(306) WEDNESDAY (الأربعاء)

(FOR HİJİR) 273 + 09/12/1436 + (FOR AD) 144 + 23/09/2015 = 4227

EXPECTED RESULT:

1443 + 2022 + (DHUL-HİJJA 9) + 753 = 4227

IT İS ALSO:

(BEİT AL-MAQDİS CONQUEST) 1135:

(DAY OF ARAFA) 411 + (PALESTİNE) 239 + (MASJİD AL-AQSA) 361 + (FOR HİJİR) 273 + (1443 G., 1808) = 4227

INTEGRATİON OF MASJİD AL-AQSA WİTH BOTH DATES

09/12/1436 + (MASJİD AL-AQSA 361) = (BLESSED LAND CONQUEST) 1818

NOTİCE: MASJİD AL-AQSA 361 + 23/09/2015 = 2408

EXPECTED RESULT:

(361) + (1808 ألف وأربع مائة وثلاث وأربعون GEMATRİA OF 1443) PALESTİNE + 239 (MASJİD AL-AQSA) = 2408

INTEGRATİON OF MASJİD AL- AQSA WİTH BOTH DATES:

(09/12/1436) + (23/09/2015) + (MASJİD AL-AQSA) 361 = 3865

EXPECTED RESULT:

+ 1808 (ألف وأربع مائة وثلاث وأربعون 1443 OF GEMATRİA)
(PALESTİNE) 239 + (BLESSED LAND CONQUEST) 1808 = 3865

INTEGRATION OF DAY OF ARAFA TO BOTH DATES:

(AD) 95 + 23/09/2015 + (AH) 218 + 09/12/1436 + (DAY OF ARAFA 411) = 4228

EXPECTED RESULT:

636 + (PALESTİNE) = 239

(OMAR'S CONQUEST İN AD) 1187 + (SALAHUDDİN'S CONQUEST) + (AD) 144 + 2022 (NEXT CONQUEST) = 4228

(PALESTİNE) 239 + (MASJİD AL-AQSA) 361 + (CONQUEST) 488 + 23/09/2015 + AH + AD + 09/12/1436 = 3817

EXPECTED RESULT:

3817 − 2416 = "…INDEED, IT IS WE WHO SENT DOWN THE QUR'AN AND INDEED, WE WILL BE ITS GUARDIAN" 1401

(G. 2022) 1401

OBSERVE CAREFULLY!

3921 = (144) FOR AD + 23/09/2015 + (273) FOR AH + 09/12/1436

USE BALANCE 3921

EXPECTED RESULT: 456 − 3921 = 3465

2022 + 1443 = 3465

INTEGRATION OF WEDNESDAY WITH BOTH DATES:

(FOR AD) **144** + 23/09/2015 + (FOR AH) **273** + 09/12/1436 + (306) WEDNESDAY = 4227

EXPECTED RESULT:

1443 + 2022 + (9 DHUL-HIJJA) 753 = 4227

IT IS ALSO:

(DAY OF ARAFA) **411** + (PALESTINE) **239** + (MASJID AL-AQSA) **361** + (BEIT AL-MAQDIS CONQUEST) **1135** + (G. 1443) 1808 + (FOR AH) 273 = 4227

INTEGRATION OF MASJID AL-AQSA WITH BOTH DATES:

09/12/1436 + (MASJID AL-AQSA) **361** = 1818

23/09/2015 + (MASJID AL-AQSA) **361** = 2408

1808 (G. 1443) + (239) PALESTINE + (MASJID AL-AQSA) **361** = 2408

INTEGRATION OF DAY OF ARAFA WITH BOTH DATES:

(DAY OF ARAFA) 411 + 23/09/2015 + **AD 95** + 09/12/1436 + **AH** 218 = 4228

NOTICE!

(OMER'S CONQUEST IN AD) 636 + (PALESTINE) **239** + (SALAHUDDIN'S CONQUEST) 1187 + 2022 (NEXT CONQUEST) + FOR AD 144 = 4228

GEMATRIA OF BALANCE 456

$1548 + 4228 = 5776$

EXPECTED RESULT: THE ESTONİSHİNG RESULT İS THAT THİS WAS THE HEBREW DATE İN 2015

HEBREW DATE CORRESPONDİNG TO **2015 AD** $= 5776$

INTEGRATİON OF WEDNESDAY WİTH HİJİR DATE:

(FOR AH) $273 + 1436 + $ (306) WEDNESDAY $= 2015$

OBSERVE CAREFULLY!

$2057 = 29/06/2022$

INTEGRATİON OF FRİDAY 9 DHUL-HİJJA

EXPECTED RESULT:

(PALESTİNE) **239** + (BLESSED LAND CONQUEST) **1818** $= 2057$

8 JULY 2022 **AD CORRESPONDS 9 DHUL-HİJJA 1443**

NOTİCE!

FRİDAY **149** + (FOR AH) $273 + 1443 + $ (753) DHUL-HİJJA 9 $= 2627$

EXPECTED RESULT:

JULY (453) $+ 8 + $ (FOR AD) $144 + 2022 = 2627$

NOTİCE!

9 DHUL (753) HİJJA + (FOR HİJİR) $273 + 1443 = 2478$

EXPECTED RESULT

(361) MASJİD AL-AQSA + 2022 + 95 = 2478

456 BALANCE + 2022 = 2478 IMPRESSİVE

THİRD SEARCH:

A SEARCH İN VERSE 124 OF SURAT AL-NAHL

THE ORDER OF THE VERSE 124, AL-NAHL = *"THE SABBATH WAS ONLY APPOINTED FOR THOSE WHO DIFFERED OVER IT. AND INDEED, YOUR LORD WILL JUDGE BETWEEN THEM ON THE DAY OF RESURRECTION CONCERNING THAT OVER WHICH THEY USED TO DIFFER"* [AL-NAHL: 124] FROM THE BEGINNING OF THE QURAN

2025 + 124 = 2149

EXPECTED RESULT:

CONQUEST 488 + 1443 + 218 AH = 2149

218 + 1443 + 488 = 2149

IF WE START COUNTING FROM THE VERSE 124 OF SURAT AL-NAHL TILL THE VERSE 45 OF SURAT AL-KAMAR *"[THEIR] ASSEMBLY WILL BE DEFEATED, AND THEY WILL TURN THEIR BACKS [IN RETREAT]"* [AL-KAMAR: 45], THE TOTAL WOULD BE 2868 VERSES.

NOTICE THE GEMATRIA OF *"[THEIR] ASSEMBLY WILL BE DEFEATED, AND THEY WILL TURN THEIR BACKS [IN RETREAT]"* IS 611

"[THEIR] ASSEMBLY WILL BE DEFEATED, AND THEY WILL TURN THEIR BACKS [IN RETREAT]" 611 + 1443 + FOR AH 273 = 1327

EXPECTED RESULT:

2022 + (276) 29 JUNE (حزيران) = 2327

NOTICE!

29/06/2022 = 2057

(PALESTINE) 239 + (BLESSED LAND CONQUEST) 1818 = 2057

NOTICE!

1436 + (FOR AH) 273 + 1443 + 9 (DHUL-HIJJA) 762 + (PALESTINE) 239 + (*WHOSE SURROUNDINGS WE HAVE BLESSED*) 1063 + (MASJID AL-AQSA) 361 = 3868

"*…SO FEAR THEM NOT BUT FEAR ME…*" [AL-BAQARA: 150] 2425 + 1443 = 3868

2022 + 1443 = 3868

SO IS THERE ANY ONE TO CONSIDER!

AFTER ALL THIS, IS THERE ANY DOUBT; I REALLY DON'T SAY 100% THAT 2022 IS A CUT-OFF DATE BUT I AM SURE THAT IT HAS A MEANING BEYOND AND I DO ATTRIBUTE 98% ON THAT.

"*…SO FEAR THEM NOT BUT FEAR ME…*" 2425 + 1443 = 3868

2022 + 1443 = 3868

A DIFFERENT SEARCH ON THE DEMISE OF ISRAEL BASED ON THE DAY OF ITS ESTABLISHMENT 18/07/1948 (JULY)

AT THE TIME WHEN ISRAEL WAS ESTABLISHED, THE DATE OF ITS DEMISE AND WE ALL KNOW THAT THE BEGINNING OF THE SECOND AND PERMANENT TRUCE DATE IS THE ACTUAL DATE OF THE ESTABLISHMENT OF ISRAEL, AND THAT WAS ON 18/07/1948.

NOTICE!

18/07/1948 + 144 (FOR AD) = 2117

IT IS 2022 + AD 95 = 2117

IT CORRESPONDS THE HIJRI DATE 12/09/1367

12/09/1367 + FOR AH 273 = 1661

THE SURPRISE IS 1443 + AH 95 = 1661

NOW, WE WILL TRY TO SUM BOTH DATES USING THE GEMATRIA OF THE MONTHS NAMES

18 + JULY 453 + 1948 + AD 95 = 2514

EXPECTED RESULT:

CONQUEST 488 + 1808 (GEMATRIA OF 1443 IN ARABIC LETTERS) + AH 218 = 2514

12 + رمضان (9TH MONTH OF AH) 1091 + 1367 + 218 AH = 2688

361 MASJID AL-AQSA + (29 JULY) 305 + 2022 = 2688

Notice the month of حزيران (June) 6, the name used in Palestine: 29/06/2002 = 2057

1818 (Blessed Land conquest) + 239 Palestine = 2057

Sum of both dates AH and AD:

18 + تموز (July) 453 + 1948 + AD + 95 = 2514 plus

12 + رمضان (9TH month of AH) 1091 + 1367 + 218 AH = 2688

2514 + 2688 = 5202

The surprise is that 5202 equals:

Masjid Al-Aqsa 361 + *"Whose surroundings we have blessed"* 1063 + 2022 + AD 95 + 1443 + AH 218 + 5202

These are some of the researches that all confirmed how this is serious and not a joke nor a guess nor dreams, thus accurate and logical data and calculations that cannot be denied but by arrogant. Subhanallah, Who says in his Holy Book: *"....and has enumerated all things in number"* [Al-Jinn: 28]. His Almighty also said: *"But all things We have enumerated in writing"* [Al-Naba: 29]

Return to the table

THE NINTH PROPHECY

Mohamed (PBUH) Prophecy

THE WHITE COLOR OF THE NABAWI MOSQUE AND ITS SPLENDOR
IS A WARNING SIGN FOR THE EMERGENCE OF DAJJAL

THE IMAM AHMAD IN HIS MUSNAD [19279] SAID: "NARRATED FROM MIHJAN IBN AL-ADRAA THAT THE PROPHET (PBUH) SPOKE TO PEOPLE AND SAID: THE DAY OF SALVATION AND WHAT A DAY OF SALVATION, THE DAY OF SALVATION AND WHAT A DAY OF SALVATION, THREE TIMES THEN HE WAS ASKED WHAT IS THE DAY OF SALVATION? HE SAID: DAJJAL WOULD COME AND GO UP TO UHUD THEN HE WOULD LOOK TO THE MEDINA AND TELL HIS COMPANIONS, YOU SEE THIS WHITE PALACE, THIS IS THE MOSQUE OF AHMED, THEN HE WOULD COME TO THE MEDINA WHERE HE WOULD FIND ANGELS EVERYWHERE THEN HE WOULD COME TO THE WASTE-LAND OF JURUF WHERE HE WOULD PITCH HIS TENT THEN THE CITY SHALL SHAKE THREE TIMES, THUS THERE WOULD COME OUT EVERY HYPOCRITE AND REPROBATE, MAN AND WOMEN AND GO FORTH TO HIM, THAT IS THE DAY OF SALVATION".

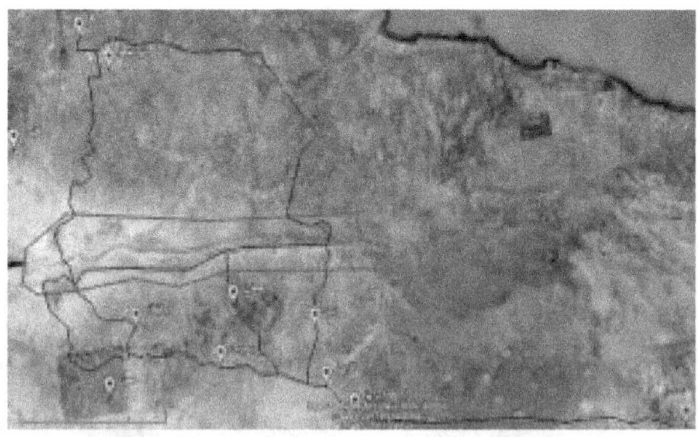

REPORTED FROM NAHEEK IBN SARIM AL-SAKUNI, HE SAID: THE PROPHET (PBUH) SAID: "YOU WOULD FIGHT THE INFIDELS UNTIL THE REST OF YOU WOULD FIGHT THE DAJJAL ON THE JORDAN RIVER, YOU ON ITS EAST AND THEM ON ITS WEST. I DON'T KNOW WHERE JORDAN WOULD BE THEN.

Narrated by Al-Tabarani and Abu Na'em "Reported from Naheek ibn Sarim Al-Sakuni, he said: The Prophet (PBUH) said: "You would fight the infidels until the rest of you would fight the Dajjal on the Jordan River, you on its east and them on its west" he said: I don't know where Jordan would be then on the Lord's land. Narrated by Yahya bin Hassan and Othman bin Said reported from Muhammad ibn Aban. [Knowledge of the Companions of Abu Na'em Part 18, p. 440].

RETURN TO THE TABLE

✹ ✹ ✹

THE THENTH PROPHECY

The Number 76 and Surat Al-Isra

EACH OF THE VERSES OF SURAT AL-ISRA ENDS WITH A WORD CALLED INTERVAL, SUCH AS: (شكورا... نفيرا... لفيفا...وكيلا ...,, ETC.), I.E. THERE ARE 111 INTERVALS. WHEN WE DELETE THE REPEATED INTERVALS, THEIR NUMBER BECOMES 76[55]. IT IS NOTEWORTHY TO RECALL THAT THIS NUMBER REFERS TO THE EXPECTED AGE OF ISRAEL IN AD, KNOWING THAT WE HAVE ALREADY FOUND OUT THAT EACH OF SURAT AL-ISRA'S WORDS CORRESPONDS TO A YEAR, AND IT IS ALSO REMARKABLE TO KNOW THAT THERE ARE ONLY (4) VERSES IS THIS SURAH WITH (19) WORDS EACH. THEN THE TOTAL IS: $(4 \times 19) = 76$

THE VERSE 76 AND THE ROOT "فزز" FEZEZ:

HERE, LET'S REFER TO THE VERSE 76 OF SURAT AL-ISRA: *"AND INDEED, THEY WERE ABOUT TO DRIVE YOU FROM THE LAND TO EVICT YOU THEREFROM. AND THEN [WHEN THEY DO], THEY WILL NOT*

REMAIN [THERE] AFTER YOU, EXCEPT FOR A LITTLE "[AL-ISRA: 76], IT IS CLEAR THAT THE WORD 'A LITTLE' IS FOLLOWED BY THE VERSE NUMBER WHICH IS 76.

THIS NUMBER MAY REFER TO THE NUMBER OF YEARS; THE PROPHECIES SOMETIMES COME IN THE FORM OF A SYMBOL THAT NEEDS INTERPRETATION, AS IN THE TRUTHFUL VISION; VISION OF YUSUF, PEACE BE UPON HIM, OR VISION OF THE KING IN SURAT YUSUF. HERE ARE INDICATIONS OF A LIKELY PROBABILITY OF THIS:

a. VERSE 76 SPEAKS ABOUT EVICTION FROM OLD COUNTRY 'HOME', AND ABOUT THE DURATION THE UNBELIEVERS REMAINED AFTER THIS EVICTION. WHAT WE ARE LOOKING AT HERE IS TO SEARCH FOR THE NUMBER OF YEARS THAT ISRAEL SPENT AFTER ITS ESTABLISHMENT IN THE HOLY LAND, AND AFTER THE EVICTION OF ITS PEOPLE FROM IT.

b. SOME MAY SAY THAT THE VERSE SPEAKS OF THE PROPHET (PBUH) EVICTION AND THIS IS TRUE, BUT THE VERSE THAT FOLLOWS IS: *"[THAT IS OUR] ESTABLISHED WAY FOR THOSE WE HAD SENT BEFORE YOU OF OUR MESSENGERS; AND YOU WILL NOT FIND IN OUR WAY ANY ALTERATION"* [AL-ISRA: 77] SPEAKS OF A WAY IN THE PAST, THE PRESENT AND THE FUTURE.

c. IN THE HOLY QURAN, ONLY THREE WORDS [56] WERE DERIVED FROM THE TRIPLE ROOT WORD 'FEZEZ'. IT IS REMARKABLE THAT THESE THREE WORDS ARE FOUND IN SURAT AL-ISRA, VERSES (64, 76, 103).

VERSE 64: *"AND INCITE [TO SENSELESSNESS] WHOEVER YOU CAN AMONG THEM…"* [AL-ISRA: 64] IS COMPOSED OF 19 WORDS AND THEREFORE, CORRESPONDS TO 19 YEARS AS WE

PREVİOUSLY MENTİONED. THE SECOND VERSE İS 76, İN WHİCH WE ARE CONSİDERİNG THE PROBABİLİTY FOR İTS NUMBER TO BE İNDİCATİNG THE TOTAL OF YEARS THAT ISRAEL WİLL STAY İN THE BLESSED LAND; İT İS A SYMBOLİC İNTERPRETATİON OF A THE WORD 'A LİTTLE'. THE THİRD VERSE İS: *"SO HE INTENDED TO DRIVE THEM FROM THE LAND, BUT WE DROWNED HIM AND THOSE WITH HIM ALL TOGETHER"* [AL-ISRA: 103] FOLLOWED BY VERSE (104): *"AND WE SAID AFTER PHARAOH TO THE CHILDREN OF ISRAEL, 'DWELL IN THE LAND, AND WHEN THERE COMES THE PROMISE OF THE HEREAFTER, WE WILL BRING YOU FORTH IN [ONE] GATHERING"* [AL-ISRA: 104]. İ.E. WE HAVE TOLD THE CHİLDREN OF ISRAEL AFTER THE DROWNİNG OF PHARAOH, DWELL İN THE HOLY LAND, [57]; THİS WAS THE DWELLİNG PROVİDED BY NECESSİTY TO ACHİEVE THE PROMİSE OF THE FİRST SPOİL, WHİCH CAUSES THE FİRST DİASPORA. WHEN THE PROMİSE OF THE SECOND AND LAST TİME COMES, WE WİLL GATHER YOU FROM THE DİASPORA, AND İN FACT YOU BELONG TO DİFFERENT ORİGİNS, UNLİKE THE FİRST TİME, WHERE YOU BELONGED TO ONE ORİGİN, NAMELY JACOB, PEACE BE UPON HİM: *"AND WHEN THERE COMES THE PROMISE OF THE HEREAFTER, WE WILL BRING YOU FORTH IN [ONE] GATHERING"* [AL-ISRA: 104]. THE REMARQUABLE HERE İS THAT THE THİRD WORD *"DRIVE THEM"* IS RELATED TO BOTH SPOILS, PARTICULARLY THE LAST ONE WHICH IS THE FOCUS OF THIS SEARCH. LET'S NOT FORGET THAT THE NUMBER OF WORDS FROM THE START OF TALK ABOUT THE PROPHECY: *"AND WE GAVE MOSES THE SCRIPTURE…"* [AL-ISRA: 2] TİLL THE LAST STRAİGHT TALK ABOUT İT: *"AND WHEN THERE COMES THE PROMISE OF THE HEREAFTER, WE WILL BRING YOU FORTH IN [ONE] GATHERING"* [AL-ISRA:

104] IS 1443 WORDS WHICH CORRESPONDS TO THE YEAR OF 1443 AH. IT IS NOTEWORTHY TO SAY THAT THE NUMBER OF YEARS FROM THE YEAR OF AL-ISRA TILL THIS YEAR IS 1444 LUNAR YEARS, I.E. (76x19).

IN LIGHT OF THE ABOVE, AND GIVING THE FACT THAT EVERY WORD IN SURAT AL ISRA CORRESPONDS TO A YEAR, HERE IS THE NUMERICAL EQUATION THAT WAS OBTAINED FROM THE WORDS THAT WERE DERIVED FROM THE WORD "FEZEZ": THE FIRST WORD (واستفزز) WAS FOUND IN VERSE 64, WHICH HAS 19 WORDS, THE SECOND WORD (ليستفزونك) IS IN VERSE 76, WHICH IS MEANT TO INDICATE THE POSSIBILITY THAT IT SYMBOLIZES THE NUMBER OF YEARS AND THE THIRD WORD (يستفزهم) IS IN VERSE 103, WHICH SPEAKS OF THE DROWNING OF PHARAOH, FOLLOWED BY THE VERSE THAT SPEAKS OF THE PROMISE OF THE HEREAFTER. THEREFORE, WE SAY THAT: AS THE FIRST VERSE IS COMPOSED OF 19 WORDS, AS EVERY WORD IN SURAT AL-ISRA CORRESPONDS TO A YEAR, AND SINCE WE ASSUME THAT THE NUMBER OF VERSE 76 REFERS TO THE NUMBER OF YEARS, THE EQUATION IS AS FOLLOW: $(76 \times 19) = 1444$; THE SURPRISE HERE IS THAT THE ORDER OF THE THIRD WORD, I.E., (يستفزهم) "DRIVE THEM", IN SURAT AL-ISRA IS (1444). SO, OBSERVE CAREFULLY!!

<u>RETURN TO THE TABLE</u>

THE CALCULATOR PREDICTS
THE DEMISE OF ISRAEL

INTRODUCTION TO THE CALCULATOR

WHEN THE PHİLOSOPHER AND THE FRENCH SCİENTİST PASCAL BLAİSE İNVENTED THE CALCULATOR İN 1642, HİS GOAL WAS TO HELP HİS FATHER COLLECT TAXES, BUT İN FACT HE HAD DİSCOVERED A UNİQUE, BEAUTİFUL AND HARMONİOUS SYSTEM THAT EVERYONE TODAY NEEDS.

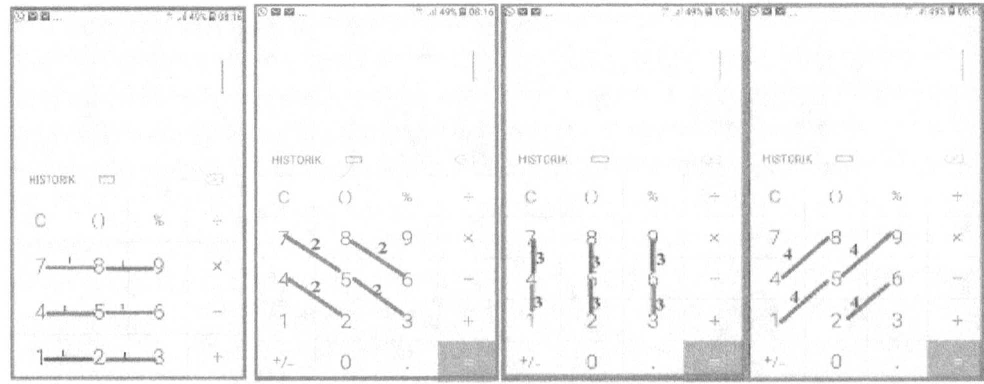

THE NUMBER SYSTEM İS DESİGNED FROM 1 --- 9 PLUS 0 İN QUADRATİC, TRİANGULAR AND ASCENDİNG FORM, UNLİKE PHONE NUMBERS WHİCH ARE A DESCENDİNG SYSTEM.

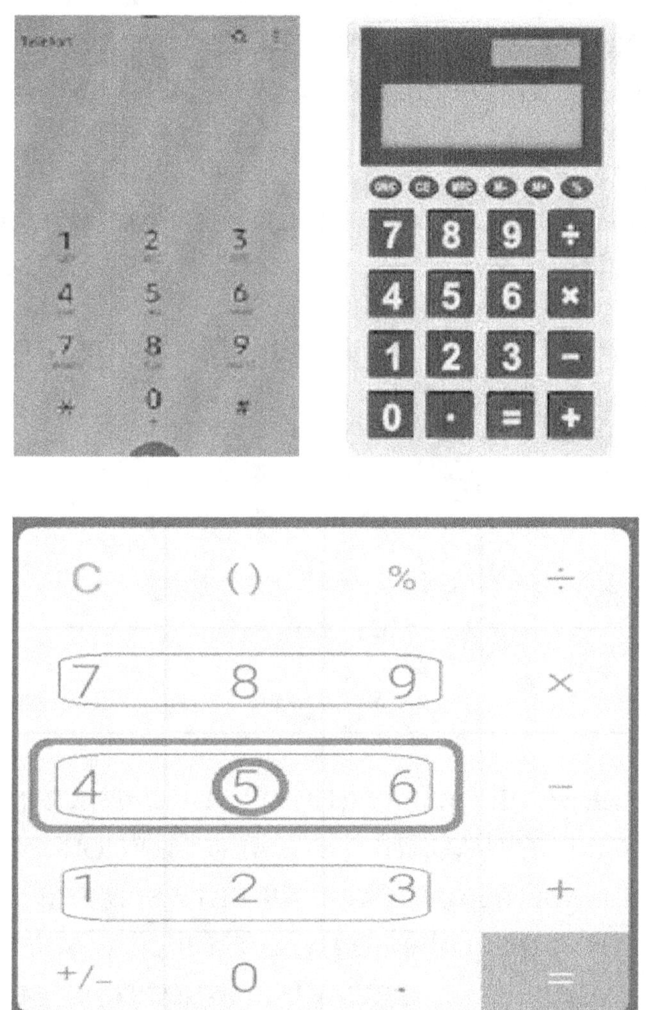

WHAT İS AMAZİNG İN THİS TRİPARTİTE SYSTEM İS WHEN YOU COMBİNE THE THREE UNİTS

$$789 + 456 + 123 = 1368$$

NOTİCE

$$1368 \div 3 = 456$$

FIRST: 456 IS THE NUMERICAL VALUE OF BALANCE IN SURAT AL-HADID WHICH WE MENTIONED PREVIOUSLY. IT WAS DISCOVERED BY DR. BASSAM JARRAR WHO WROTE A BOOK ABOUT IT TITLED BALANCE 456.

SECOND: İT İS İNDEED A BALANCE BECAUSE İT MEDİATES THE THREE UNİTS.

THİRD: THE NUMBER 5 İS THE MİDDLE OF THE NUMBERS FROM 1 TO 9 OT 0 TO 10.

$$4 + 5 + 6 = 15$$

$$15 \div 3 = 5$$

$$1 + 2 + 3 + 4 + 5 + 6 + 7 + 8 + 9 = 45$$

$$45 \div 5 = 9$$

THESE ARE SOME OBSERVATİONS; THE İMPORTANT THİNG NOW İS TO EXAMİNE 9 MATHEMATİCAL EQUATİON TO CONSİDER İF THERE İS A MATHEMATİCAL LİNK BETWEEN THE SYSTEM İN THE CALCULATOR DİSCOVERED BY THE FRENCH SCİENTİST PASCAL BELİZE AND THE PREVİOUS AND UPCOMİNG ISLAMİC CONQUESTS İN JERUSALEM, WHİCH WAS REFERRED TO BY DR. BASSAM AL-JAJJAR AND THEN THE RELATİONSHİP OF THE NUMBER BALANCE 456 WİTH THESE 3 CONQUESTS

EQUATIONS:

- FIRST EQUATION:

$654 + 789 = 1443$ WHICH IS THE HIJIR DATE FOR THE YEAR 2022

- SECOND EQUATION:

$789 + 654 + 123 + (\text{BALANCE})\ 456 = 2022$ WHICH IS THE LIKELY AD DATE FOR THE DEMISE OF ISRAEL AND THE START OF THE SECOND UNIVERSALITY OF ISLAM.

- Third equation:

Salahuddine's conquest 27/rajab/1187 AD corresponding to 583 AH

$789 + 963 + 321 + 147 = 2220$

$27 +$ GEMATRİA OF((RAJAB رجب) $205) + 583 +$ GEMATRIA OF (HIJIR) $218 + 1187$ **AD** $= 2220$

- FORTH EQUATION:

CONQUEST OF OMAR BIN KHATTAB (GOD BLESS HIM)

IS THE SUM OF THE NUMBERS HORIZONTALLY FROM RIGHT TO LEFT MINUS THE SUM OF THE NUMBERS HORIZONTALLY FROM LEFT TO RIGHT I.E. REVERSED.

$$123 - 456 - 789 - 321 + 654 + 987 = 594$$

WHICH IS THE GEMATRIA OF (MASJID AL-AQSA) $361 + 15$ (OMAR'S CONQUEST) $+ 218$ (HIJIR) $= 594$

- FIFTH EQUATION:

9 MOVES ON THE CALCULATOR FOLLOWING THE NUMBERS FROM 1 TO 9

$$741 + 852 + 963 + 321 + 123 + 456 + 654 + 987 + 789 = 5886$$

IT IS THE TOTAL OF THE THREE CONQUESTS OF BEIT AL-MAQDIS IN AD AND AH

1. FIRST CONQUEST: BY THE KHALIFA OMER BIN KHATTAB, GOD BLESS HIM, IN THE YEAR 15 AH CORRESPONDING TO 636 AD.

2. SECOND CONQUEST: BY SALAHUDDINE AL-AYYOUBI IN THE YEAR 583 AH CORRESPONDING TO 1187 AD.

3. NEXT CONQUEST, GOD WILLING: I THINK IT WOULD BE BY IMAM MAHDI MOHAMED BIN ABDULLAH IN THE YEAR 1443 AH CORRESPONDING TO 2022 AD.

THE TOTAL: FIRST CONQUEST + SECOND CONQUEST + LIKELY NEXT CONQUEST EQUAL THE TOTAL OF PRECEDENT 9 MOVEMENTS $= 5886$

$$15 + 636 + 583 + 1187 + 2022 + 1443 = 5886$$

- SIXTH EQUATION:

- ITS RELATIONSHIP WITH JERUSALEM

TOTAL OF 9 ARITHMETIC MOVES ON THE NUMBERS FROM 1 TO 9, BUT THE ACCOUNTING IS FROM BOTTOM TO TOP STARTING BY THE 7TH MOVE. THE TOTAL RESULT IS: 4104

Notice:

What is the order of the verse 4104?

Starting from the last verse in Quran from Surat Al-Nas, rear order

The answer:

""*And We said after Pharaoh to the Children of Israel, 'Dwell in the land, and when there comes the promise of the Hereafter, We will bring you forth in [one] gathering*"[Al-Isra: 104].

This indicates without any doubt that there is a relationship of this verse with our subject, the demise of Israel and the number 4104.

Observe carefully the following expressions and their Gematria!

Gematria of (Beit Al-Maqdis 1135) + Gematria of (Masjid Al-Aqsa 361) + Gematria of (Whose surroundings We have blessed 1063) + Gematria of (2022 in Arabic letters 1401) + Gematria of (For AD 144) = 4104

- Seventh equation:

Equation 5886 minus Equation 4104 = 1782

IT IS THE DATE OF SALHUDDINE, GOD HAVE MERCY ON HIS SOUL AND BLESS HIM, 10/02/1187 AD + 583 AH = 1782

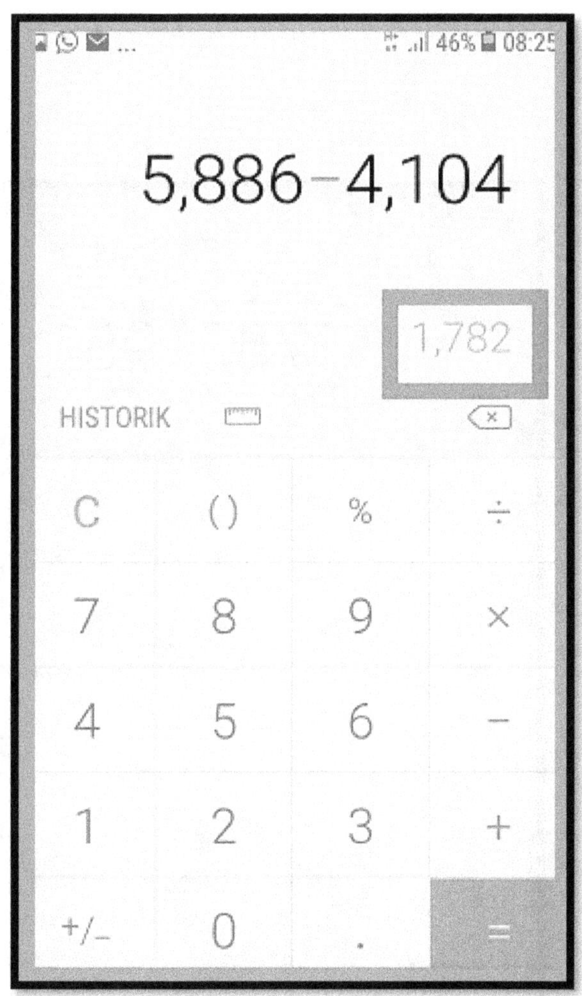

- EIGHTH EQUATION:

CUTTING OFF AND SECTIONED (753 + 951) = 1704

THIS IS THE GEMATRIA OF (*AND WHEN THERE COMES THE PROMISE OF THE HEREAFTER*)= 1704

- NINTH EQUATION:

THE PREVIOUS EQUATION 1704 MINUS 159 = 1545 WHICH IS THE GEMATRIA OF (2022 IN ARABIC LETTERS 1401) + GEMATRIA OF (FOR AD) 144

1704 − 159 = 1401 + 144 = GEMATRIA OF 2022 AD

CONCLUSION

THE EQUATIONS ARE AWESOME, DENSE AND UNCOMPROMISING. WHO WANTS MORE, JUST REFER TO DR. BASSAM JARRAR, DIRECTOR OF THE NOON INSTITUTE FOR QURANIC STUDIES IN JORDAN, GOD PRESERVE AND BLESS HIM, THE EDITOR OF THE ORIGINAL RESEARCH.

ALL OF THEM PREDICT THAT THE EVENTS OF THE AL-AQSA MOSQUE AND ITS GEOPOLITICAL LOCATION ARE VERY IMPORTANT AND HAVE NO PARALLEL IN THE WHOLE LAND; LAND OF RESURRECTION, LAND OF UNION, LAND OF ISRA AND MIRAJ, IT IS THE LAND BLESSED BY ALLAH FOR ALL WORLDS.

ALMIGHTY SAYS: *"AND WE DELIVERED HIM AND LOT TO THE LAND WHICH WE HAD BLESSED FOR THE WORLDS"* [AL-ANBYA: 71].

IT SHOWS ALSO THE CENTRALITY OF JERUSALEM NOT ONLY IN THE WORLD, BUT IN THE WHOLE UNIVERSE AND THEREFORE WE FIND THE ANSWER TO THE FOLLOWING QUESTIONS:

WHY MUHAMMAD, PBUH, WAS ASCENDED FROM JERUSALEM TO THE HEAVENS ABOVE AND TO COMMUNE WITH HIS LORD AT THE PRESENCE OF ALLAH AND NOT FROM OTHER HOLY PLACES?

WHY DID GOD GATHER THE SOULS OF THE PROPHETS AND MESSENGERS ALL NIGHT OF ISRA AND MIRAJ TO PRAY BEHIND MUHAMMAD, PBUH, IN MASJID AL-AQSA OVER OTHER MOSQUES?

WHY IS THE LEVANT TO BE THE PLACE WHERE ALL CREATURES ARE RESURRECTED FROM ALL OF THEIR GRAVES AND FROM WHICH THEY SPREAD? IT WAS NOT WITHOUT IT.

THE ANSWER: THE PROPHET (PBUH) SAID IN SAHEEH HADEETH, WHICH WAS NARRATED BY IBN HUWALAH: "GO TO SYRIA, FOR IT IS ALLAH'S CHOSEN LAND, TO WHICH HIS BEST SERVANTS WILL BE GATHERED, BUT IF YOU ARE UNWILLING, GO TO YOUR YEMEN" AL-ALBANI, SUNAN ABI DAWUD: 2483.

FOR THIS REASON, GOD, THE ALMIGHTY, MADE THE EVENTS COINCIDING WITH THE MOVEMENT OF THE UNIVERSE FROM THE STARS, THE SPHERES AND ALL CREATIONS, FROM HUMAN, JINN, NIGHT, DAY, WIND, RAIN, AND THE SMALL OR LARGE OF HIS CREATURES, ALL IN HIS PLAN AND BOOK; IN A HARMONIOUS AND IMPLICIT WAY INSIDE THE VERSES OF THE QURAN IN A PRECISE NUMERICAL AND ARITHMETICAL SYSTEM WHICH SECRETS BEGAN TO BE DISCOVERED IN SUCH STUDIES AND I ASSUME THAT SOON THE DISCOVERIES IN THIS AREA WILL BE VERY USEFUL FOR AN EXTRAORDINARY SCIENTIFIC RISE, SURPASSING THE AGE OF TECHNOLOGY.

ALMIGHTY SAYS:

"THAT HE MAY KNOW THAT THEY HAVE CONVEYED THE MESSAGES OF THEIR LORD; AND HE HAS ENCOMPASSED WHATEVER IS WITH THEM AND HAS ENUMERATED ALL THINGS IN NUMBER" [AL-JINN: 28].

GOD IS AWARE OF EVERYTHING, OWNS EVERYTHING AND THE KORAN, IS HIS ALMIGHTY BOOK IN WHICH RELAY THE WHOLE UNIVERSE' SECRETS, IT HAS THE KEYS TO ALL SECRETS AND THE HAPPINESS OF ALL HUMANKIND REGARDING THEIR RELIGION AS WELL AS LIFE .

Almighty says: *"And if there was any Qur'an by which the mountains would be removed or the earth would be broken apart or the dead would be made to speak, [it would be this Qur'an], but to Allah belongs the affair entirely"* [Al-Ra'd: 31].

This is an invitation for young Muslims to start research as individuals, groups and institutions in order to get into the research and understanding of the Quran's endless secrets, knowing that the Quran comes on the Day of Resurrection as the first time as it bears abundant knowledge and fewer are those who knows about it. The Messenger of Allah, May peace and blessings be upon him, said: «The Qur'aan comes on the Day of Resurrection, as if it had not been touched.. »

It is also an invitation to Islamic countries to frame efforts and monitor the funds and possibilities so as to give greater efficiency, wider and faster benefit; God only knows.

Return to the table

CONCLUSION

THE UNSEEN İS KNOWN ONLY BY ALLAH AND THE CERTANİTY OF AN EVENT İS ONLY CONFİRMED WHEN İT OCCURS. IF WHAT İS MENTİONED İN THİS BOOK İS TRUE, THEN İT İS WİTH THE HELP ALLAH, BUT İF İT İS WRONG, THEN İT İS FROM MYSELF. I İNVİTE YOUNG PEOPLE AND RESEARCHERS TO FURTHER GO THROUGHOUT THE SCİENCES OF THE QURAN, ESPECİALLY THE GEMATRİA. ALMİGHTY SAYS: *"WE HAVE NOT NEGLECTED IN THE REGISTER A THING"* [AL-AN'AM: 38]. HOW İT CANNOT BE AND İT İS THE BASİS OF ALL SCİENCES AND THE SOURCE OF GUİDANCE AND KNOWLEDGE. ALMİGHTY SAYS: *"AND IF THERE WAS ANY QUR'AN BY WHICH THE MOUNTAINS WOULD BE REMOVED OR THE EARTH WOULD BE BROKEN APART OR THE DEAD WOULD BE MADE TO SPEAK, [IT WOULD BE THIS QUR'AN], BUT TO ALLAH BELONGS THE AFFAIR ENTIRELY"* [AL-RA'D: 31]...

I THİNK THAT THE FUTURE İS VERY AUSPİCİOUS FOR ALL PEOPLE, AND THAT MANY OF OUR JEWİSH BROTHERS WHO HAVE HATH WRONGED US WİLL SOMEDAY BELİEVE THAT THE WHOLE LAND BELONGS TO ALLAH, HE SHALL GİVE İT TO WHOMEVER HE WİLLS, MAKE WHOM HE WİLLS DWELL İN İT, TAKE İT FROM WHOM HE WİLLS AND ALL OF THAT İN A TERM. ALMİGHTY SAYS: *"AND FOR EVERY NATION IS A [SPECIFIED] TERM. SO WHEN THEIR TIME HAS COME, THEY WILL NOT REMAIN BEHIND AN HOUR, NOR WILL THEY PRECEDE [IT]"* [AL-A'RAF: 34].

NO ONE HAS TO BE TEMPTED BY HİS POWER, ALLAH İS THE STRONGEST, THUS ALLAH İS THE STRENTGH İT SELF, BUT YOU WİLL BE AFLİCTED BY ONE ANOTHER, THOSE WHO BELİEVE WİLL BE RECOMPENSED AND THOSE WHO DİSBELİEVE WİLL BE HATH

BELİGHTED; ALLAH GİVE TİME BUT DOES NOT NEGLECT. THAT MUSLİMS LİKE GOOD AND WELL-BEİNG OF ALL AND LOOK FORWARD TO COOPERATİON AND SYNERGY WİTH ALL TO FİGHT EVİL, POVERTY AND DİSEASE, AND PROVİDE WHATEVER İS İN THE PUBLİC AND PRİVATE İNTERESTS. JEWS SHOULD KNOW THAT SAFİYYAH BİNT HAYY IBN YAKHTTAB, MAY ALLAH BE PLEASED WİTH HER, THE WİFE OF MUHAMMAD, PBUH, WAS OF JEWİSH ORİGİN AND WAS TİTLED BY QURAN BEİNG THE MOTHER OF EVERY MUSLİM; ALMİGHTY SAYS: *"THE PROPHET İS MORE WORTHY OF THE BELİEVERS THAN THEMSELVES, AND HİS WİVES ARE [İN THE POSİTİON OF] THEİR MOTHERS. AND THOSE OF [BLOOD] RELATİONSHİP ARE MORE ENTİTLED [TO İNHERİTANCE] İN THE DECREE OF ALLAH"* [AL-AHZAB: 6], NOT TO MENTİON MANY GOOD COMPANİONS AND RESPECTED GENTLEMEN OF JEWİSH ORİGİN. WE MUSLİMS DO NOT DİFFERENTİATE BETWEEN MOSES, JESUS AND MUHAMMAD, MAY PEACE AND BLESSİNGS OF ALLAH BE UPON THEM ALL, WE LOVE AND RESPECT THEM. LET THEM ALSO KNOW THAT THE TRUE JUDAİSM THAT MOSES, MAY PEACE BE UPON HİM, CAME WİTH İS ISLAM.

REFERENCES

1. HOLY QURAN
2. NOON CENTER FOR QURANIC STUDIES
3. QURAN GEMATRIA V2 PROGRAM, ACCESSIBLE THROUGH THE LINK: HTTP://WWW.ANGELFIRE.COM/CO4/DOCTORHANI

KINDLY FOLLOW THE ABOVE STEPS:

FIRST:

AFTER DOWNLOADING THE PROGRAM ON THE COMPUTER, ACTIVATE IT ONCE AS TO TAKE IT PLACE ON MY COMPUTER

THEN SEARCH FOR IT INSIDE THE DISC C UNDER PROGRAM FILES

THIS IS HOW IT LOOKS LIKE: QURAN GEMATRIA V2

AFTER THAT, PUT A SHORTCUT OF IT ON THE DESKTOP TO ACCESS IT WHEN NEEDED

DO NOT FORGET TO PRAY FOR THE DESIGNER OF THIS PROGRAM AS INDICATED WHEN RUNNING IT

SECOND:

How to run the program: it starts by copying the words that needs to be calculated with Gematria, placing and pasting them on the program then activate the latter by clicking the word ((ok)) so as to give in a few seconds the Gematria of the word or phrase required. Please consider the privacy of the Quran during application and review it before use.

Return to the table